The Secret of Parenting

Anthony E. Wolf, Ph.D.

ILLUSTRATIONS BY THE AUTHOR

FARRAR, STRAUS AND GIROUX

NEW YORK

The
Secret
of
Parenting

How to Be in Charge of Today's Kids

—from Toddlers to Preteens—

Without Threats or Punishment

Farrar, Straus and Giroux
19 Union Square West, New York 10003

Copyright © 2000 by Anthony E. Wolf, Ph.D.
Distributed in Canada by Douglas & McIntyre Ltd.
Printed in the United States of America
First edition, 2000

Library of Congress Cataloging–in-Publication Data

Wolf, Anthony E.
    The secret of parenting : how to be in charge of today's kids—
from toddlers to preteens—without threats or punishment /
Anthony E. Wolf ; illustrations by the author.—1st ed.
        p.   cm.
    ISBN 0-374-52708-3 (alk. paper)
    1. Parenting. 2. Child rearing. 3. Parent and child. I. Title.

HQ755.8.W642 2000
649′.1—dc21   00-026443

Parts of this book originally appeared in *"It's not fair, Jeremy Spencer's parents let him stay up all night!" A Guide to the Tougher Parts of Parenting*

To Mary Alice, Nick, and Margaret

Contents

Contents

Contents

Acknowledgments

This book was edited by Patty Bryan. Her skill and intelligence are reflected throughout the pages that follow.

I would like to thank Mike Bryan for his editing work, Elisabeth Kallick Dyssegaard for her help with this book as well as her unwavering and much appreciated support over the last ten years, and Joe Spieler, who by seeing some promise in what I wrote is responsible for my having a career as a writer.

I would also like to thank my two regular readers, my wife, Mary Alice, and my friend Hugh Conlon, both of whom have been extraordinarily generous in listening to, looking at, and commenting upon the book as it evolved.

I would also like to thank Tim Scussell for his kindness in making me welcome at his two McDonald's restaurants—where most of this book was written.

Last, I want to thank Wendy Friedman and Diane Nadeau for their help in typing the many drafts of this manuscript.

Introduction

"I never would have talked to my parents that way."

You hear this all the time from parents, and they're right. Children talk and act worse with their parents today than children did in the past. And as recipients of their children's sometimes incredibly bratty behavior, many parents conclude that *they*, the parents, must be doing something wrong. Yet the main reason that children today talk back more and are less obedient is not because parents are doing something wrong. It's because they're doing something right.

The reason kids act worse today goes back to the revolution in child raising that began a half century or so ago. That revolution had important and far-reaching ramifications. I introduce it with a quick scenario.

Eight-year-old Jimmy comes to school and on his face is the clear imprint of a hand.

"Where did you get those marks, Jimmy?" asks his teacher. "My mom hit me," answers Jimmy.

Introduction

Sixty years ago, the teacher might well have replied, "I'll bet you deserved it." Today, by law, in every state of this country, the teacher must report such an incident to local child-abuse authorities. At the heart of the revolution in child raising is the fact that the more severe forms of punishment, such as hard slaps across the face, the use of a belt or a hickory switch, or being locked in one's room for extensive periods of time, are now considered unacceptable. Parents and psychologists got the idea that if real fear and harsh punishment were removed from the arsenal of child training, children would develop into better, happier, and kinder adults. This was an important and wonderful and correct idea, but it has caused one major problem: without the threat of harsh punishment hanging over their heads, kids are fearless, unlike children of generations past, and feel free to fuss and complain and make their parents' lives miserable.

In past generations, children knew there was a line over which *they* could not go. They were afraid of the punishment they would receive. Even when the punishment was not physical, children were afraid of the unknown and unspoken consequences of their actions. Today's children have a sense that there is a line past which their *parents* are not allowed to go, even if they are not exactly sure where that line is. They know at a very early age about something called "child abuse."

"I never would have talked like that to my parents."
"What do you think would have happened if you had talked back?"
"Oh, I didn't want to find out."

The elimination of harsh punishment carried with it one great unknown: how will children who were not afraid of their parents act? Now we know.

"Brendan, would you please take the glass out into the kitchen?"

"Why?"

"Because I'm asking you to, that's why."

"But it's not my glass."

"TAKE OUT THE GLASS!"

And then Brendan, grumbling, takes the glass into the kitchen. "Why do you always make me do stuff? Jennifer never has to do anything."

A direct and unquestionable result of the elimination of harsh punishment from the parenting arsenal is that children today talk back more and do not obey as quickly as did children of previous generations. In an attempt to regain some of the control lost with the elimination of harsh punishment, most parents turned to threats and lesser punishments.

"Jared, stop kicking the table *or you're not going outside to the Playspace.*"

These seemed to work—sort of—but they also seemed to have very little effect on the back talk or do much to produce the *immediate* obedience that springs from the fear of harsh punishment. With or without the mild threats, Jared and most kids today are probably not going to comply immediately or without a certain amount of mandatory fussing.

Although children no longer meet the standard for compliance that only the fear of harsh punishment can produce, parents have and always will have sufficient power and leverage to produce children who behave most of the time as we want them to. This power comes from the automatic child-to-parent love attachment. And because this attachment is so deep-seated, the power that arises from it is *more* than enough to achieve all the goals of parenting. Furthermore, this power and leverage *never* depended upon kids being afraid of their parents. It only seemed that way. Parents have great power with their children, separate from any leverage based on fear. They just need to learn how to use what they have.

It is good that harsh punishment is no longer an acceptable part of the parenting repertoire, because it only creates controls based exclusively on a fear of what others will do to you. All that harsh punishment ever taught children, and all it ever will teach children, is to avoid getting caught. It does nothing to help children develop the inner controls that prevent them from acting badly because those actions cause suffering to others. It does nothing to develop the true conscience we want our children to have, that we want everyone to have. In fact, harsh punishment gets in the way of this maturing process.

And, very important, punishment—any punishment—devalues human suffering, simply because it is the intentional infliction of suffering. Parents are those individuals in a child's world who are supposed to represent the side of good. When they intentionally inflict suffering, the implicit message to the child is that suffering must be a legitimate means to an end. Punishment as part of child-raising practice teaches the child that human suffering is not an *absolute* harm.

What if it were possible to raise good, civilized children without having to punish them? What if punishment is simply not necessary in order to raise civilized children who become civilized adults? Why would you then want to use punishment?

I can only say that this is how I was raised. It is how my children were raised. This book invites you to try as well. I focus on what I consider to be the most difficult part of parenting: what to do when you are going against the wants of your children, when you must say "no," when you want them to stop doing something, or when you want them to do what they don't feel like doing. This book offers a way of parenting without threats or punishment that not only produces children who become good and civilized adults, but also eliminates so much of the fussing that accompanies raising today's kids. I offer a way to bring back the joy of parenting.

I

Why They Act
As They Do

1

Baby-Self Basics

Seven-year-old Steven comes home from school. He opens the door, takes off his coat, and, not a foot away from a coat hook that conveniently sits on the wall directly next to the door, drops his coat on the floor.

"Steven, how many times do I have to tell you to hang up your coat?" says his mother exasperatedly as she enters the room to greet him.

"I don't know. A lot?" mumbles Steven as he then, with great effort, hangs up his coat.

The next day when Steven comes home from school, he enters the house and immediately takes off his coat. On this particular day, his mother, who only the day before had yelled at him for not hanging up his coat, happens to be standing right by the door.

"Hi, Mom," says a happy Steven as he simultaneously drops his coat on the floor.

How many times will Steven's mother have to tell him to hang up his coat before he learns? Many. Since he's now in second grade, a rough calculation of years left in school times the number of days a year he will come home and drop his coat on the floor comes to ten times about two hundred, which is many, many times.

However, the rest of this story has an odd twist. Steven has a cubby at school and in that cubby is a coat hook. Every day, without anybody saying anything to him, Steven neatly hangs his coat on the coat hook in his cubby. Not all second graders regularly hang up their coats in school, but many who never hang up their coats at home do it at school without a second thought.

I use this story because it's a simple example of a phenomenon that is true of all children, all adults, everybody. Each of us has two separate and distinct modes of operating—in essence two separate selves.

One of them is mostly an at-home self and I call it the *baby self*. This self and how it acts is defined by two overlapping and overwhelming characteristics: the baby self must be fed and fed *now*, and it has zero tolerance for any form of stress. The baby self feeds itself by indulging, collapsing, relaxing, unwinding—soaking up all the good stuff. A perfect meal for the baby self would consist of lounging on the couch, eating Doritos, with headphones blocking out any unwanted interruption. The baby self gets stressed when it has to do something that it doesn't feel like doing at any given moment. Being asked to take out the trash while it's lounging on the couch would qualify as major stress. This zero tolerance is often the part of the baby self that parents understand the least, and it's also the part that causes the most trouble. Baby selves can be nice and lovable, but when they're asked to tolerate any form of stress, they can get very cranky and crabby.

The other mode, which I call the *mature self*, exists mainly in the world outside the home. Unlike its baby-self counterpart, the mature self is willing to work, will tolerate stress, has patience, has self-control, and can and is willing to delay gratification. It will work toward a goal. Steven's mature self hangs up his coat at school.

These separate modes come and go during the course of a day, very much like the changing of gears. You can actually feel the switch. Take me, after a hard day at the office. Let's say I've come home from a very stressful day during which I was able to hold it together completely. Throughout the day, I was patient, mature, and professional—at all times. When I arrive home, even as I open the front door, I can feel the energy draining out of my body. I stagger into the house, stumble forward, barely able to make it to the couch, where I collapse, hardly able to move or talk. If I'm lucky, the remote control for the TV is within arm's length. If it is not, I may need assistance.

Couples know this phenomenon. Perhaps one family member has been home for the whole day and has not talked to another adult during that time. When his or her partner, who maybe has talked to *too many* adults during the day, arrives home, he or she is not as eager to launch immediately into a conversation as the one who has been isolated at home all day.

"You would not believe what happened with the man who was supposed to come and fix the refrigerator leak . . . "

But the partner, now fully in baby-self mode, does not want to hear about it. Listening requires patience and patience is just another form of stress. What many couples, in fact, learn to do is to give the one just coming home a certain amount of down time, in effect giving that person's baby self some time before initiating a conversation with the mature self.

"*Now* tell me about your day."

All baby selves are the same, with no variation from person to person over the course of a lifetime. The mature self grows, gradually taking over more of the day-to-day functioning, ultimately coming to control the where and when of our baby selves. But baby selves never change.

We All Need Our Baby Selves

When my children were little, I loved them very much, of course, but I also remember how I loved them best of all when they were asleep. They were so cute. Anyone who has young children knows that moment when they are finally in bed and asleep. At last it is your time—your *own* baby-self time. At last you can do what you feel like doing. Understandably, when you at last have a chance to be by yourself and relax, you consider it an intrusion when a small pajamaed figure quietly shuffles into the room.

"Can Grandma Edith who died see me in my room?"
"No. Go to bed."
"But I can hear her breathing."
"You can't hear her breathing. GO TO BED."
"You come with me."
"*GO TO BED.*"

A striking example of children's need for enough baby-self time can be seen in a well-known phenomenon with foster children. Many of these children join a new family and are quite well-behaved for the first month or two. But then, for no apparent reason, they start acting badly. The "honeymoon period" ends and the true test of the foster placement begins. Will the foster parents hang in there with the children who are going to give them trouble, or, as often happens, will they call the agency and request that the children be placed with another family?

The well-behaved foster children who suddenly turn unruly are a common occurrence, but from one perspective it doesn't make sense, because the laws of psychology say that if a behavior is rewarded it will continue. If the children were behaving well and, as a result, were getting a lot of positive feedback from their foster parents, why wouldn't they continue to be good? The answer is that the mature self may have been getting lots of positive feedback for being good, but the baby self was starving. Being on good behavior meant operating in the mature mode. This is very much like being a guest in the home. That kind of behavior, especially if you are a child, can only be sustained for so long. Eventually the needs of the baby self take over.

It is in the baby-self mode and only the baby-self mode that we, our children—all of us—receive our basic, deep nurturing. I liken this nurturing of the baby self to a boxer who comes back to his corner between rounds, collapses on his stool, gets replenished, which sustenance then allows him to go back into the ring. With children, this deep nurturing feeds the core of the personality, and it is upon this deep nurturing that all else is built. It is the base that allows them to grow and mature and ultimately go out and deal with the world.

When we adults have to do without our baby selves, the stress of everyday life becomes just too much and we cannot cope. We all need a place for our baby selves. But our children, because they are still so young, need it even more.

Who Gets the Baby Self?

An absolute fact of human psychology is that the mere physical presence of a parent brings out the baby self in a child. It's not a conscious decision on the part of a child. It simply happens. If you want to see the classic example of this, take a story all parents know.

Valerie had been over at a friend's house. As soon as her mother arrives to take her home, Valerie starts up.

"Can we go to McDonald's before we go home?"

"No, dear, I'm sorry. I told you we're not going to have time."

"But why, why can't we go?"

"I already told you. There's not enough time."

"But why? You promised. You never do anything I want. Why?"

"Valerie, I didn't promise anything."

"Yes, you did. You did. You're a liar. You promised. You promised!"

Watching this scene unfold, the other child's parent looks on with surprise.

"I don't understand. Valerie was so well-behaved until you showed up. She and Alexa were playing really well together."

Both parents then incorrectly conclude:

"Oh, she must be tired."

Wrong. Had Valerie's mother showed up an hour earlier or an hour later, the same thing would have happened.

Another example:

Have your child or children go to a restaurant with another couple. Videotape the scene. Then take your kids with you to that same restaurant. Videotape this scene. You will then have matched recordings of the mature- and baby-self behavior of your children. And what happens if you *and* the other couple together accompany your kids to the restaurant? The baby self usually wins.

"Oh, we've never seen this side of your kids before."

Even years later, when adults visit their own parents, maddeningly the baby-self side still comes out.

"I don't understand it. As an adult I've learned to deal with so many difficult people, but when mother starts up, I go crazy."

More accurately, it is not strictly a parent who brings out the baby self in a child. Anyone with whom a child has a strong love attachment, who is involved in regular day-to-day child care, and with whom a child feels totally safe and comfortable, will bring out the baby self. Hence with grandparents from a distant city whom the children see at most a couple times a year, only the mature self makes an appearance. But grandparents who regularly participate in day-to-day child care will see much of the baby self.

The same distinction can even apply with the parents themselves. If both are involved in regular day-to-day child care, both will get the baby self. But if one parent does much of the day-to-day child care and one does little, one gets the baby self, the other the mature self. And there's no question who gets which.

Parents Bring Out the Baby Self

"Luke, stop playing with the lamp switch," says his mother to her seven-year-old son.

"I'm not hurting anything. I'm just experimenting."

"Luke, stop playing with the lamp switch."

"I'm not doing anything. Why do you always yell at me about stuff?"

"I don't always yell at you."

"Yes, you do. You yell at me about everything."

Meanwhile, Luke's father, who is in the next room reading his newspaper, is disturbed *again* by the yelling between his wife and son. Disgustedly, he gets up from his chair, goes into the next room, and says:

"Luke, stop playing with the lamp switch."

Whereupon Luke immediately stops. At that point Luke's father turns to his wife and says something that has probably caused a number of divorces:

"Claire, you just aren't tough enough with the kids."

I'll show you what's tough, thinks Luke's mother as she considers reaching for the lamp and throwing it at her husband. And she's right about the injustice of the accusation. Luke's very different responses with his two parents have nothing to do with toughness, and everything to do with the simple fact that his mother gets Luke's baby-self version and his father the mature-self version.

Who gets the baby self has nothing to do with the sex of the parent. I have known families where the mother worked out of the house and most of the day-to-day child care was handled by the father. In those families, the father got the baby self, the mother the mature self.

Which Is the Real Self?

Which of these two versions—the baby self, which parents mainly encounter, or the mature self, which, for the most part, the outside world sees—is the truer indicator of who a child *really* is and, more important, who this child is going to become as an adult? Let me give a couple of examples.

Garrett's mother and father were dreading their first conference of the year with Mrs. Millbrook, the first-grade teacher of their regularly tantruming six-year-old son.

"What's your secret?" bubbled Mrs. Millbrook. "Garrett's such a polite boy, and he's my best helper."
"We're Mr. and Mrs. *Anderson*."

"Yes, Garrett Anderson. He's one of my shining stars."
"He is?"

Another story:

When fifteen-year-old Danielle was at home with her parents, she was everything you wouldn't want in a daughter. She was self-centered, always gave her parents a hard time when they asked her to do anything, and when she spoke, she did so with a particularly snotty tone. One weekend her parents went away and Danielle stayed at her friend Sara's house for the weekend. Two weeks later Danielle's mother ran into Sara's mother.

"You must be so proud of your Danielle," said Sara's mother.
"Danielle who?" asked Danielle's mother.

But they were, of course, talking about the same child. Sara's mother went on.

"She was so polite, and she offered to help, (which they really do at other people's houses) and you know, she's such an *interesting* girl. Why, at supper she talked so intelligently about the refugee problems in Southeast Asia."

Returning home, Danielle's mother confronted her daughter.

"Why can't you act that way with us? We're the ones who care about you the most. We're the ones who have sacrificed to give you a good life. Why? Why can't you give us the behavior that we deserve?"
"Because you're mean," replied Danielle, as usual giving her mother the full baby-self treatment.

The Baby Self Obeys Its Mother

Which is the real Garrett Anderson; which is the real Danielle? The answer is, absolutely, the mature-self version. The proof comes later. By the end of adolescence, as their children move into young adulthood, parents start to see more and more of the mature self (though perhaps never completely). Not only do their children become nicer, and more respectful to their parents, but they do go out into the world and become good citizens. It does work that way. It is the mature-self version of our child that is the far better indicator of what they really are and who they will become.

So what does this say about the baby-self behavior that parents endure at home for years and years? First, it *does not* say that you are doing something wrong as a parent, or that there is something wrong with your child. What it says is that this is just the way it is, the natural progression from baby self to mature self when children have no fear of harsh punishment.

Look at it this way: what better place is there than a home for the baby self to rant and rave? If there has to be this place of nurturing, where at times your child can be extremely unpleasant, very babyish and very childish, wouldn't you rather it be your own home rather than out there with the rest of the world?

Being stuck with the baby self at home leads to what is really a double standard for parenting.

I don't like, I don't enjoy, and I want to see as little as possible of the bratty side of the baby self. But because I want the baby self in my house and because I am allowing it by not resorting to harsh punishment, I am also accepting that I will get some of the baby self's bratty side.

You do best by having two separate standards of behavior that you will expect from your kids. You then gear your reactions to their behavior accordingly. You will have one standard—a much more demanding code of behavior—when out in the world, away from home and family, and a lesser standard at home.

Even where this double standard is unspoken, today's children know that it exists, and they abide by it, for the most part. It doesn't even present a problem for them, because it fits the reality of what's going on inside them: baby self at home and with parents, mature self away from home and family.

In the Mind of the Baby Self—Nothing Counts

The realm of the baby self is a world of its own, and the wild inconsistencies in what the baby self does and says can be most difficult for parents to comprehend. The degree to which the baby self can be seemingly oblivious to what is going on in the rest of its life leaves parents baffled. But for kids, it's not a problem. The words and actions of the baby self are not based on rational considerations, but on how the baby self *feels* at this moment, and especially on how it hopes its words and actions will affect its parents. Deeper truths are completely irrelevant to the baby self, and easily denied. The baby self lives only in the moment. Nothing else counts. So when parents try to get across to the baby self the consequences of its actions, the baby self doesn't see the point. That was then, this is now.

"I hate you. I do. I hate you. I wish I had a different mother. Anybody but you. I really mean it. I hate you."

Suddenly, out of nowhere, we appear. We hook Lawrence up to a lie detector.

"Lawrence, is it true that you really hate your mother?"
"Yes," answers a glaring Lawrence.

The lie detector shows that he is telling the truth. But later that day while Lawrence is quietly playing a game with his brother, we again appear and again hook him up to the lie detector. We repeat our question:

"Do you really hate your mother, Lawrence?"
"No, of course not," says Lawrence, looking at us as if the question is rather stupid. Again, the lie detector shows that he is telling the truth.

So, which is the truth? Either Lawrence hates his mother or he doesn't. Of course, Lawrence does not hate his mother. He felt angry, he *felt* that he hated her at the time, but he does not actually hate her.

Another example:

"I didn't. I didn't take it. I didn't take her stupid Baby Ruth," screams Raymond.

However, the chocolate is still on his hands and face. What is going on in his head? How can he possibly think that his parents will believe him? But Raymond not only feels certain that his parents *will* believe him, but also believes at the moment he is screaming that he is, in fact, completely innocent.

Or:

"I don't care what my room looks like. I hate my room. I hate living here. I hate this house. I do. We should get a new house."

The funny thing is, Lorenzo's abhorrence for his home only surfaces when he is made to clean up his room. The rest of the time, he loves the house and especially takes great pride in his room and the way it is decorated. He even picked out the color of the wall paint himself.

Or:

"How was your day at school?" asks Brittany's mother as her daughter climbs into the car.
"Terrible. And it's too hot in my class and Mrs. Trenchler isn't fair and Suzy Weiderman is a big jerk," whines Brittany, launching into a string of complaints about school, just as she always does as soon as she gets into the car.

Brittany's mother is at a loss when her daughter complains like this, because the larger reality is quite the opposite. Brittany likes school a lot, she thinks Mrs. Trenchler is the best teacher she has ever had, and she and Suzy Weiderman talk on the phone every night for an hour and will undoubtedly do so tonight as well. But Brittany's baby self enjoys an after-school unwinding fuss, and in its throes her baby self colors her day anyway it feels like.

I need to mention that even with adults the baby self doesn't "count." But, obviously, this arithmetic gets far more complicated in adulthood. Lovers and spouses, by the nature of the relationship, bring out the baby self in each other. But it doesn't work to feel totally free to say whatever one wants all of the time.

"Carla, you're so stupid. I can't believe some of the things you say. It's just like the stuff your mother says all the time."

Maintaining a successful adult love relationship requires a balancing of the baby-self's needs with the mature-self's restraint and judgment. Not always an easy task.

So how is it possible for children, and even adults, to say things based on their hoped-for effect and to truly believe them at the time, while not really meaning them at all? When you look carefully, you'll see that the mature self and the baby self exist in their own realities. They are fully aware of each other. They are both "me." But the emotional connection between the two often is just not there. Truly, in this respect, each of us is something of a split personality.

Ivana is a perfect example. One day as she was eating lunch with her closest friends at school, her friends began teasing a ten-year-old boy with a serious learning disability. Her friends actually went so far as to call him a "retard." Ivana was shocked and actually stood up to her friends, telling them that what they were doing was wrong. For a twelve-year-old to stand up to her friends in that way took real courage. Later that day at home, Ivana, still deeply disturbed by the incident, recounted to her mother how her own best friends had acted in such a cruel and heartless manner.

Now, wouldn't you know that this same Ivana happened to have a ten-year-old brother named Reggie who, wouldn't you know, happened to have a severe learning disability? And, wouldn't you know, she regularly teased him, most frequently calling him "retard," which she especially enjoyed because it so effectively seemed to drive Reggie crazy?

"Ivana," said her mother after hearing her daughter's story, "I can't believe you're saying this to me. You call Reggie a 're-tard' all the time. How can you possibly be upset at your friends when you do exactly the same thing every day?"

Ivana's answer was the same as any child would give:

"It's not the same."
"Ivana, that's ridiculous. Of course it's the same."
"No, you don't understand. It's *not* the same. *He's my brother.*"

I should also point out that baby selves have a common understanding about things that happen in this world of their own. Reggie probably is very sensitive about his learning dis-ability and the word "retard" would cut him deeply had an-other child applied it to him. But though he hates when his sister calls him a retard, and has a fit when she does so, it is the teasing and not the word that drives him crazy. Reggie knows this name-calling is in the realm of the baby self, and it does not count. Ivana and her words are part of home and family and they aggravate but mean little.

For children, the unspoken lines between the two do-
mains are an automatic part of their lives. To them, that's just
how it is. If they see themselves as considerate, honest, and
hardworking when they are out in the big world, the fact that
they are inconsiderate, dishonest, and lazy when at home is
just not a problem. Though they can intellectually appreciate
the inconsistency of their behavior, they cannot *feel* it. More-
over, they don't understand why their parents don't see things
in the same way.

Does this mean that everything children say is total nonsense? Not at all. But when confronted by upsetting statements or actions from their children, parents need to ask
themselves, *When am I hearing this?* If what their child is saying or doing comes at a time when she is not getting her way
and the baby self is in charge, parents need to think long and
hard before they take it too seriously.

2

❖

The Piggyness of the
Baby Self

When it comes to parents, the baby self wants as much of them as it can get, endlessly, passionately. I often picture the baby self's craving for its parents like those pictures of chicks in a nest with their mouths open—total craving. This incredible piggyness of the baby self when it comes to parents is not in doubt. Let me tell a story that I'm sure will sound familiar to every mother and father.

Seven-year-old Robert is sitting on the floor in the same room as his father, playing with a set of building blocks. He is totally engrossed in what he is doing and for the past twenty minutes has not glanced up once at his father, who is chopping vegetables for soup. Suddenly Robert drops what he is doing and starts pestering his father. Why? The answer, known to all parents, is that his father has answered the phone.

"Dad. Dad."
"What is it, Robert? I'm on the phone."

"Dad, look at what I'm building. Isn't it good?"
"Robert, I'm on the phone."
"But, Dad, Dad, you have to look at it."

Or:

"Dad, I want some orange juice."
"Robert, I'm on the phone. Can't you get it yourself?"
"No, I'm afraid I'll spill it." (Robert has never in his life worried about spilling orange juice.) "I need you to do it."
"Robert, I am on the phone."
"But, Dad, I want orange juice."

Or, of course, the same exact thing would happen should his five-year-old sister, Tracy, quietly come into the room. Her mere presence, standing there, saying nothing, would immediately trigger the same response.

"Dad, Dad."

What is Robert's problem? The answer is the mindless piggyness of the baby self. When it was just Robert and his father alone together in the room, the baby self was content. Playing with the blocks was fun, and Robert was having a good time. He had no interest in his father at that time, mainly because his father was potentially available. But the piggy baby self always keeps a watchful eye because *should* it want its father, its father must be immediately and totally available. Once his father was on the phone or once his sister was in the room, his father's immediate and total availability was in jeopardy. Those circumstances were not acceptable to the baby self.

The same often happens when a child is well-behaved when alone with one parent. If the second parent comes in, the baby self feels its access to full attention is threatened. The child starts misbehaving or pestering one of the parents, because the baby self worries that the two adults might pay attention to each other. What about me? Baby selves, in regard to their parents, want everything.

Prize #2

What makes the piggyness of the baby self so important in regard to parenting is that when the baby self is not getting its way, it will do *anything* and say *anything* to correct that problem. The baby self has no conscience. Should it fail to get its way, the baby self will always go after prize #2, which is as passionate and as endless an amount of you as it can get.

Eight-year-old Mary Jean says to her father, "Dad, can I have a Popsicle?"

I want to go back to what I talked about at the beginning of this book in regard to the removal of harsh punishment from child raising. That change was part of the excellent idea that it was good to be nice to children—that not so much what they were taught, but more how they were dealt with was what determined who they would become. As part of this—was it so crazy?—people thought that if parents treated their children completely kindly, fairly, compassionately, *reasonably*, that their children would respond to them in a similar manner. Now I want you to notice how Mary Jean's father speaks to his daughter.

"I'm sorry, honey, but supper's only twenty minutes away and you know, in the past, if you've had a snack before supper, it's ruined your appetite and you hardly eat anything at the meal. So, I'm sorry, sweetheart, but no you can't have a Popsicle."
"Gosh, Dad, you're right. I really had wanted a Popsicle.

But it's true. Every time I have something to eat this close to supper, it does spoil my appetite. So, shucks, I guess I'll just have to wait a little longer until supper's ready. No harm in asking though, huh, Dad?"

There is an unconfirmed story that on March 18, 1977, a child from Cedar Rapids, Iowa, responded in this manner. Though as I said, the report is unconfirmed. You're probably more familiar with another kind of response.

"Please, please, just this one time. Please. Please, I'm sooo hungry. Please."

"No, I'm sorry, Mary Jean."

"But I'm really hungry. It's not my fault supper's in twenty minutes. I can't wait that long. My stomach's rumbling. Listen to it."

"I'm not going to listen to your stomach, Mary Jean. You're just going to have to wait."

"But I can't wait. I'm too hungry."

"Mary Jean, supper is in twenty minutes."

"But that's too long. I'm so hungry now.

"I'm sorry, Mary Jean."

"But I never get anything I want. I don't."

"You know that's not true, Mary Jean."

"Yes, it is true. And Brendan gets everything."

"Brendan doesn't have anything to do with this."

"Yes, he does. You give him everything and I can't even have a little Popsicle."

As long as her father continues to participate, Mary Jean will go on forever because the baby self cannot let go.

Or eleven-year-old Babette to her father:

"Dad, can I go over to Stephanie's house after supper? We have a project for school that we're working on."

"No, I'm sorry, Babette. You were out last night. It's a school night and you know you still haven't completely gotten over your cold. Not tonight."

"But, Dad, you don't understand. I have to. You don't understand. Stephanie's counting on me."

"Well, I'm sorry. You'll just have to try to do it on the phone."

"But, Dad. You don't understand. You can't do this. You just can't, Dad!"

"No, I'm sorry, Babette. And I don't want to hear anymore about it."

Babette's father then does what is exactly the right thing to do. He turns and walks away. But, if he has a typical eleven-year-old girl, he will hear more about it. Babette will follow him throughout the house. Should her father go into a room and close and lock the door, Babette will stand outside, face pressed against the door, continuing her assault.

"But you don't understand. You have to give me a reason. You didn't give me a good reason. Why? Why? You don't understand. Why?"

At that moment, we appear:

"Excuse me."

"What? Who are you? Where'd you come from?"

"Do you mind if I ask you two questions?"

"I don't know. I guess not."

"Do you think your father is going to change his mind?"

"No, he's an idiot."

"Then if he's not going to change his mind, how come you're still standing here talking to him in this ridiculous position, with your face pressed against the door?"

And, if totally honest, Babette answers:

"I don't know."

But we know. The baby self hates separating from you above all. It hates separating even more than it hates not getting its own way. Babette, in the full clutches of the baby self, will not let go of her father.

What the Baby Self Hates (More Than Anything Else in the World):
Absence of You

You know this feeling. In arguments, especially with someone with whom we are very close—spouses, lovers, even with our children, when our own baby self more readily comes to the surface—the baby self cannot let go, cannot let matters drop. In these arguments, the voice of the baby self sounds like, "I have to get her to see my way." "I have to make her understand." "We have to get some resolution to this." In the course of such arguments, the baby self does not want to separate—ever. And sometimes with arguing adults where both baby selves are too much in the forefront, the arguments can end up with serious negative consequences, not as a result of the content of the argument, but purely because neither side separated, and it went too far.

The phenomenon of the baby self gets worse. Not only will it not let go, it unmercifully *provokes*. It actually custom tailors, learning by trial and error, what tactics will drive you berserk. Baby selves, using the same brain as mature selves, are extraordinarily skilled at knowing how to push your particular buttons. To anything you might say, they will always have a comeback, which more often than not escalates the fussing to higher and higher levels. As long as you stay involved, they will drag you along with them. When children are not getting their way, they feed on parental response—*any* response.

This insatiable desire that kids have for parental response leads to the secret of parenting.

When you are going against the wants of your children, you should do what you have to do, say what you have to say, and then end it. Decide fast, stand firm, and disengage fast.

Just let me give you this classic example.

Eight-year-old Vinnie had been pestering his mother about going to the store in order to get him a new action figure. Vinnie's mother felt that he had plenty of action figures, and after a brief discussion she sought to end the matter.

"No, Vinnie. No more action figures. That's it."

From prior experience, Vinnie knew that when his mother used that particular tone of voice, nothing further he could say or do would get her to change her mind, nor would he be able to suck her into another endless baby-self argument. So he turned to leave. Any time you have gone against the wants of your children and they then turn and leave, you have done excellently, for the absolute last thing that the baby self ever wants is to separate, and the baby self dies hard. As Vinnie turned, now no longer facing his mother, and started to walk away, his baby self made one last desperate attempt to re-hook his mother.

"Fat jerk," mumbled Vinnie under his breath.
"What did you say?!"

Vinnie then made a full 180 degree turn and, now *facing* his mother, mumbled:

"Nothing."

But inside Vinnie, his baby self raised its fist in triumph and cried out, "YES!" His mother had snapped at the bait.

"Vinnie, I heard what you said and I do not want you talking to me that way. That is unacceptable."

Now, I am not saying that Vinnie's mother was wrong to respond to Vinnie's parting shot. But one must understand what is going on. Once Vinnie's mother said "no" about not getting him another action figure, anything else that she says or does only pours fuel on the fire. Anything further is food for the baby self—no more, no less.

"I do not want you talking to me that way."

"I can talk any way I want. You can't tell my mouth what to do."

As tempting as it might be for Vinnie's mother to respond to this latest volley from Vinnie, she must not say:

"No, Vinnie, I am your mother and I am telling you that as long as you live in this house, you may not talk to me in that manner."

No. Absolutely not. Because Vinnie's baby self is now laughing hysterically with glee and will always have a comeback.

"I don't care. I'll call Benjamin. His mother said I could live at their house. I'm going to call him now and she'll come and get me. Now you'll be the sad one."

If, after taking a firm stand, your child does or says something that you truly feel needs to be addressed, do it later, at a neutral time when the original issue has been laid to rest.

"Vinnie, the way you spoke to me this afternoon when I said 'no' about the action figure, that was not okay. It is not okay for you to talk to me that way. I do not want you talking to me that way again."

Letting Them Get Away with It

But you can't just do nothing. If you do nothing about it, they're going to feel that they are getting away with it.

No, they will not. When you are going against the wants of your children, you are always dealing with the baby self.

And because it is the baby self who is listening, the message that your children get is exactly what you want.

When I am not getting my way, anything further that I do or say:

- *Is not going to get my parents to change their minds and*
- *Is going to get nothing further from them—other than their absence.*

Deciding fast, standing firm, and disengaging fast plays tough and will get this message across to the baby self. It is definitely not what the baby self wants to hear. The more you do this, the easier it gets, because the success reinforces itself. The bottom line—and it is an absolute bottom line if you are dealing with human children—is that if you want to get less fussing, you should respond less. The more you respond, the more fussing you will get. It is an absolute rule. It is a fact. Only the fear of harsh punishment can do better.

A Two-Sided Message

Deciding fast, standing firm, disengaging fast, and not using harsh punishment also give your child another message.

Sometimes I don't like your baby self's behavior, and I will not let it rule me. However, you risk nothing serious by letting your baby self come out. Though I might not always like your baby self, I will live with it.

This two-sided message says to your child that though the baby self may not always get its way and may at times need to be controlled, it is not bad and does not need to be stamped out. And this statement teaches the profoundly important lesson that all of the flawed, impulsive, babyish parts of children are not bad, but are just a part of being a child, of being human. As a result, children grow into adults who are not alienated from all the babyish, childish stuff within themselves. They accept these as a part of being human, and they can accept these same flaws in others. Others are human, too, just like me. This simple message allows children to have a *childhood*. It is this two-sided message that is the essence of successful parenting.

Furthermore, if you truly believe that your child's obnoxious, bratty, selfish baby-self behavior is simply what baby selves do, then you won't feel the need to take all of your child's more obnoxious behavior so seriously. You can see it for what it is. With this perspective, by not having to respond to each piece of bratty behavior that your children throw at you, you are doing absolutely the most powerful thing that you can do, short of harsh punishment, to reduce the amount of fussing that you endure and to make your own job so much easier. The more you respond to baby-self fussing, the more of that baby self you will get. The less you respond, the less you will get at that time and in the future.

Letting Them Grow Up

So if I allow the baby self, do they ever grow up?

"Roderick, would you please pick up your coat from the floor."

"I can't," says forty-two-year-old Roderick from his usual reclining position on the couch. "It's too hard. My arm hurts. Besides, the bowl of Crispy Doodles is empty. I need more. Hurry!"

After picking up his coat, Roderick's seventy-four-year-old mother hobbles off on her arthritic knees to get her son more Crispy Doodles.

So that they don't turn into giant adult baby selves, kids must develop their mature selves as well. Adequate nurturing provides the early base that allows them to grow. But to make sure that as adults they have self-control, have the ability to do what they don't feel like doing, and possess the willingness to take on the responsibilities of adult life, they need more. For this they need our help.

For one, kids need to have ever increasing demands made of them. As they get older they must learn to do for themselves.

"My socks. I can't do it. I can't get my stupid socks on. You do it."

"No, Nadia, you can do it."

"No, I can't. It's too hard. I hate my stupid stocks."

Anyone who has watched a young child struggling to put on his or her socks knows that it is amazing how all children persevere and ultimately are able to succeed. Most parents instinctively know this, and rightfully expect their children to do more and more on their own as they get older, but some do too much for their kids on a regular basis. Doing too much for them can retard the process of maturity. But, as I said, most parents know better.

"Cut my meat."

"No, Randall, I know it's hard, but I'm not going to do it for you. You're going to have to cut your own meat."

"But I can't."

"Well, I guess you'll just have to try."

Or:

"Tell the lady what kind of ice cream you want."

"No, you tell her."

"If you want ice cream you'll have to speak up yourself."

Kids do need to learn to do for themselves.

Equally important, the baby self must not rule. If it always gets its way, how will children learn self-control, the ability to tolerate, patience—the hallmarks of maturity? Therefore, parents must be willing at times to say "no," to stand by their decisions and not allow themselves to be bullied by their own children.

Last, children as they get older must increasingly have a part of their lives separate from home and family, a second life that pulls out their mature self and forces them to meet responsibly the increasing demands of the world out there. They must learn that one day they will have to survive out in that world on their own.

If I want to keep friends I can't have tantrums all the time when I don't get my way, like I do at home.

I'll fail in school if I don't do any work and never pay attention.

They do care about the world out there. A part of all children strongly wants to mature and to successfully become a part of the world that is separate from their homes and families.

I want to have friends. I want to do well. I want to have a life. I don't want to stay home and be a baby forever.

To teach their children responsibility, parents must give it to them. Parents must have their children do for themselves and have them deal with the normal frustrations and disappointments of day-to-day living, and parents must increasingly put their children out there in the world, where ultimately they will have to sink or swim on their own.

Why Parenting Can Be Tough

Love them, but gradually push them to be more independent and guide them on the road to maturity. It all sounds fairly straightforward and would be relatively easy if not for the baby self. It has other plans. Lurking deep inside all children is a part that does not want to grow up at all. The deepest desire of all baby selves is to move backward to a total state of babyness, to a time when it could achieve total babyish bliss—total pleasure, total abandon, no stress, all of you, everything now. This urge to regress doesn't always come to the fore, but it is always there.

But what the baby self wants and what it *needs* are two different things altogether. All it needs is love and nurturing, and a loving, caring parent supplies more than enough of that. But what the baby self wants is everything. And for the baby self to get all that it wants would retard emotional growth. Baby selves want more than they need.

How this struggle of wills plays out in day-to-day child raising is what the rest of this book is about. In the following chapters I will describe the basic techniques of punishment-free parenting, starting with the decision-making process itself and then moving into the most difficult part of parenting, when you are going against the wants of your children.

Here you have the three basic interventions:

1. "No!" You are not going to let them have what they want.
2. "Stop!" You want them to stop what they are doing.
3. "Do!" You went them to do what they do not feel like doing.

With each of these interventions, I will describe the overall rules and then show how they play out in specific examples. I will point out the baby self's many tactics for disrupting what you are trying to accomplish, and show how you can counter these subterfuges. If you follow the rules, my secrets for parenting will become yours as well.

What the Baby Self Needs: A Lot of You

What the Baby Self Wants: All of You

Baby-Self Album 1

The Baby Self Picks Up Its Shirt

The Baby Self Gracefully Accepts Not Getting Its Choice of Restaurant

The Baby Self Passes the Salt to Its Father

The Baby Self Admits Its Guilt

The Baby Self Shares

The Baby Self *Finally* Understands

The Baby Self Listens to Reason

II

How to Do It

3

How to Make Decisions

A characteristic of human nature is that when something does not go your way, the speed with which you get over the disappointment, the speed with which you can leave it behind and move on, is directly related to how certain you are that *nothing* is going to change the situation. If you think that there is a chance, hope springs eternal. Witness a classic example.

"No, Denise, I do not want to see you again. Ever. Our relationship is ended. Period. That's it. I am now hanging up." Click.

See. I knew there was a chance. I knew it. This time he didn't say "definitely ended," like he did last time. He only said "ended." I think he's weakening.

Children cling to the most wispy of hopes. When you make decisions that go against their wants, you have to be firm and the decision-making process cannot be dragged out over time. The longer and less firm the process, the more you will bring out the baby self in your kids. Decisions must be made quickly. Once you decide, you must not back down.

Decide Fast

If you don't decide fast, you risk that your child will go on begging forever, until he or she finally wears you down.

"Mom, can I have another cookie?"

"No, Helena, two is enough."

"But, please, Mommy, please. Just one more. Please."

"Well, if I let you have one more, will this definitely be the last?"

"Oh, it will, Mommy. I won't ask for another. I promise."

"I don't know, Helena, you've said that before and then you kept pestering me."

"You'll see, Mommy, this time will be different. Please. Just this time. I've learned my lesson."

"Helena, I really would like it if you would just settle for the two cookies."

"But, Mom, I'm so hungry. I will settle for two cookies next time, you'll see."

"Helena, I don't like you always asking for more."

"I'll never ask again, I promise. Just this one time. One little cookie? Please."

"Why can't you ever accept 'no' for an answer?"

"Please. Just one. Just one. That's all I'm asking. Just one."

"Oh, all right! But you know you really drive me crazy sometimes. Here, have the cookie. But this really better be the last time."

"Oh, thank you, Mommy. You're the best mommy in the whole world. I love you so much . . . Can I have another cookie?"

It's okay to change your mind, but only if you do it swiftly.

"Mom, can I have another cookie?"
"No, Helena, two is enough."
"Please, Mom, please. Please. Just one more."
"Oh, okay,. But just one."

You can even give in to your kid's arguments.

"Can I have another cookie?"
"No, Helena, two is enough."
"But you said supper was going to be a lot later tonight. And I'm going to get real hungry."
"Oh, okay Helena. You can have another."

But beyond listening to your child's initial argument, you proceed at your peril if the decision-making process starts to get drawn out. When you make a decision that your child does not like, you want to listen, but not for very long.
But what if you can't make up your mind right away?

"Mom, can I sleep over at Diana's on Saturday night? Her mother says it's okay."
"I don't know. I'll have to think about it."
"What kind of answer is that? What's the problem?"
"I said I'll think about it."
"But why not? When are you going to tell me?"
"Lindsey, I said I'll think about it."

Even though it's not a final answer, it's a good and firm one. It is making the decision that you will not decide now. And if you end the discussion at that point, not letting Lindsey pester you into making a decision that you are not ready to make, you accomplish what you want. You have brought a swift end to the decision-making process. If and when you choose to, you will return to the question. But for now, the matter has been closed.

But what if I make the wrong decision? If I decide too quickly, won't I sometimes decide incorrectly? What if I make decisions I'll regret later?

You can postpone a decision, but most day-to-day decisions need to be made at the time, and swiftly. Two major facts of child raising are that you cannot always be right and you will make mistakes. As parents, we have the responsibility of making a life for our children, which means making a thousand decisions, day in, day out. It is just not humanly possible to consider everything judiciously, to listen to everyone, to expect ourselves to be totally wise and fair and not to make mistakes. It cannot be done. Our effectiveness as parents lies not so much in the absolute wisdom of our every decision, but in our comfort and confidence in our role as decision maker in our children's lives. We cannot always be right, nor do we need to be.

"You didn't let me have another cookie and it was a terrible mistake. I died."

"You didn't die. You're standing here talking to me.

"No, I'm in heaven and this is only a representation of my body."

Stand Firm

Perhaps the toughest rule with decision making is that once you decide, you must stand firm. It is a disaster for all when children can regularly wear down their parents and get them to change their minds. You see the real risk in allowing children to become giant baby selves. This happens not when you

Once You Have Truly Decided, You Have to Stand Firm

give them too much, but when you *give in* too often. When children are too successful at bullying their parents into getting their way, their baby selves have too much control, and this retards the emotional development of the mature self.

In the convenience store Justin wanted some bubble gum.

"No, Justin, no gum."

"Please. Please. Please."

"No, I am sorry, Justin."

"Please. Please. Just one time. Please. Please."

"No, Justin. No gum."

And then Justin, overly tired and probably needing a nap, really started fussing, eventually working himself into a full-fledged tantrum.

"I want gum. I want gum," sobbed Justin, now literally rolling on the floor in despaired, desperate outrage.

But this is where Justin's mother, having taken a firm stand, has to stay with her decision, has to be willing to see this test of wills through to the end. The battles where you have taken a firm stand are the battles that count, that you do need to win. And you *will* win them if you stay with your decision. Justin's mother's ability to endure the tantrum—no matter how far Justin takes it—says to him, *You may misbehave, but your behavior will not change anything*. That is the key point: *their* behavior cannot change *your* decision.

Pick Your Battles

Standing up to a full-scale, no-holds-barred, drawn-out tantrum can be very wearing. This means that if the place or timing is wrong, or you're simply not up to going the whole round, do not get into the battle in the first place.

Arnold's mother had had a *very* hard day. Just before supper, her four-year-old son came up to her in the kitchen.

"I want a piece of candy."

Normally, Arnold's mother would have said "no." She did not like to give Arnold snacks before supper. But Arnold had had a long, hard day as well, and his mother knew by his tone of voice that if she said "no," she was in for a big one—a prolonged tantrum. And she was just too tired. She really didn't feel like riding out the storm. She just didn't have the patience or energy for it.

"Guess what, Arnold?"
"What?"

"You're so lucky. It's National Candy before Supper Day. It only comes once a century. You get to have candy before supper."

"I do?"

And Arnold's mother, with feigned perkiness, gave her son a piece of candy.

But didn't Arnold's mother make a mistake, wasn't she allowing herself to be bullied by the potential threat of a tantrum? Wasn't she thereby playing directly into the hands of Arnold's baby self? Wasn't she going against one of her standing rules?

Had Arnold's mother taken a stand against the candy she might not have had the patience to withstand one of his huge temper tantrums, and she might have caved in finally. The tantrum would have worked, which would have been a disaster.

Or, worse, Arnold's mother might have blown up at him.

"I've had it with your tantrums. When are you going to learn to accept 'no' as an answer? I have had it with you, Arnold."

Arnold's baby self licks its lips and will most assuredly come back another day for more. It won big time, getting the special, passionate feeding that it so adores.

Also, consider where you are before going into battle. At the home of an elderly aunt, where Arnold's mother *really* does not want him to throw a tantrum, she'll be wise to let him have the candy. Or maybe in the car at the start of the dreaded once-every-four-months, three-hour, all-interstates car ride to Grandma Baba's, where there is no way of putting distance between oneself and the tantrum thrower, where we cannot say:

> "That's it, Arnold, get out of the car."
> "You're going to leave me here on the interstate?"

Let him have the candy.

Pick Your Battles

Consistency

WHAT? Doesn't all that you've just said break a basic rule of good parenting? Isn't it essential that parents be consistent? If you have a rule, don't you have to stay with it no matter what?

No. The idea that rules must always be consistent is not correct. Rules are good, and we should try to stay with them, but sometimes the greater wisdom is to make an exception. More important than the consistency of rules is, again, your firmness as a decision maker. Your ability to stand firm once you take a stand makes it clear that you, not your child, are in charge here. What must be consistent is that once you do decide, nothing your child says or does is going to change your decision.

4

"No"

How to Say It

As soon as you have made a definite decision that you are going to say "no," that you are going against the wants of your child, there's only one thing to do: deliver the news and then get out of there as fast as you can—the earlier and faster, the better. In other words:

When you are going against the wants of your children, do not feed the baby self.

"Hello, Mrs. Wildner?"
"Yes?"
"Is your refrigerator running?"
"What are you talking about?"
"Well, try and catch it before it runs away."
"Who is this?"
"This is Freddie Froody." (*Snicker, snicker, giggle, giggle*)
"I don't know any Freddie Froody. Is this some kind of a joke?"

"No, it's not a joke. It's a coke." (*Giggle, giggle, snicker, snicker*)

"A what?"

"A doke."

"I know what you are doing. You're just making a prank call."

"Oh, no, Mrs. Wildner, I'm an operator for the president of the United States. If you hold the line, he'll be on in a minute to talk to you." (*Giggle, giggle, ha, ha*)

"Whoever this is, if you keep making prank calls you're going to get in big trouble."

"*You're* going to be in big shrubble." (*Snicker, snicker, giggle, giggle, ha, ha*)

"You'd better stop this this instant."

"Here's the president. Hawo, this is the president." (*Snicker, ha, ha, ha*)

"You'd better cut this out."

"I can do what I want. I'm the president." (*Giggle, giggle, ha, ha, roar, ha, ha, roar*)

"Now, you listen here —"

"Now, you listen squeer." (*Roar, ha, ha, ha, ha, roar*)

As everyone knows, the only response to a prank call is to hang up fast. The longer you stay on the line, the more you give the caller what he or she wants, and the more likely you are to get prank calls in the future.

"I'm sorry, James. No more candy."

"But why?"

"Because you've had enough."

"No, I haven't. I want more."

"I said 'no.'"

"But why?"

"I just told you why."

"But why?"

"Don't get fresh with me or you're going to start losing television privileges."

"But why? It's not fair. I never get anything I want."

Am I saying that the same rules apply for both examples? Yes. Baby selves feed on parental response, and the less you give them of a response, the less you get of the fussing. Once you have committed to going against the wants of your child (or any baby self, for that matter, including another adult's), the faster you disengage, the lesser the chance that more fussing will ensue. After your disengagement, your child's baby self has nothing more to feed off of. Therefore, there's no opportunity to build up a full head of steam and pull you into an unnecessary bad scene. Most really bad scenes are the result of allowing a confrontation to go way past a reasonable time limit.

In short, I recommend disengaging as soon as you recognize that your child is *starting* in on a baby-self fuss. In practice, this can seem rather abrupt, almost a little harsh. But actually, it is a clear and firm statement to your child's baby self.

Don't even start.

But how do you actually do it? Here are two examples, in each of which the parent says "no" but then gets caught up in baby-self fussing, contrasted with the same complaint met with early disengagement. You will see how early in the discussion parents need to disengage.

"Mommy, can I get another rabbit?"

"No, I'm sorry Daryl, dear, I think Mr. Frisky was enough."

When Children Are Not Getting Their Way

"But, Mom, you'll see. I'll take care of it this time." (Mr. Frisky died of starvation.)

"No, Daryl. I really don't want another rabbit."

"But it won't be your rabbit, it will be my rabbit."

"No, Daryl, no more rabbits."

"But that's not fair. I said I would take care of it this time. You're not even giving me a chance."

"It's not a question of chances, Daryl. I don't want any more rabbits."

"But I never get anything I want."

"You know that's not true, Daryl."

"Yes, it is true. I don't get anything I want and Tracy gets everything she wants. She got that new bike."

"Tracy's getting a bike has nothing to do with your getting a rabbit."

"Yes, it does. She gets anything she wants and I never do. I don't."

"Tracy does not get everything she wants."
"What about her goldfish? What about her goldfish?"

Better:

"Mommy, can I get another rabbit?"
"No, I'm sorry Daryl, I think Mr. Frisky was enough."
"But, Mom, you'll see. I'll take care of him this time."

Right now—very early—Daryl's mother should end it.

"No, Daryl, I really don't want another rabbit."
"But it won't be your rabbit, it will be my rabbit."

Daryl's mother should say no more. She has already said all she needs to say.

Another example:

"Mom, will you give me another quarter for the gum machine? Carly got a prize and I didn't."
"No, I'm sorry, Christopher. Just one quarter for each of you."
"But Carly got a prize and I didn't."
"Well, you don't always get a prize."
"But it's not fair. Carly got a prize. I want another chance. All I got is a stupid gum ball. Please, just another quarter."
"No, I'm sorry, Christopher. Each of you got your quarter."
"But Carly won a prize. It's not fair. You have two more quarters. I saw them."
"Christopher, you don't always win a prize at those machines. That's just the way they work."

"But how come Carly got a prize?"

"She was lucky."

"But it's not fair then. I want another chance."

"Christopher, why can't you just accept that you can't get everything you want?"

"Because it's not fair."

Better:

"No, I'm sorry, Christopher. Just one quarter for each of you."

"But Carly got a prize and I didn't."

"No, I'm sorry, Christopher."

"But it's not fair. Carly got a prize. I want another chance. All I got was a stupid gum ball. Please, just another quarter."

Silence. Christopher's fussing should fall on deaf ears. Though Christopher's mother may feel bad for him, she cannot always make up for all of the smaller tragedies that life hands out. Christopher will survive the disappointment.

The beauty of learning to disengage is that, as hard as it may be to do, as hard as it may be to believe in, it works. We have difficulty disengaging because our natural instinct is to do just the opposite, but success reinforces itself, and the disengagement gets easier and easier to do. Once you begin to recognize the baby self lurking behind so much of what your kids do, it becomes abundantly clear that this is the only course to take.

Stay on the Subject

Confronted by a "no" and by the failure of their basic argument, baby selves adeptly try to pull parents back into the argument by changing the subject. Watch out. This is often a successful ploy. Typically, the baby self brings in what may be real issues that, however, have nothing to do with the subject at hand. This ploy is easy to recognize from the outside looking in, but not so easy to recognize when you are caught right in the middle of it.

"Dad, can I go over Mari's?" (Mari lives two houses away.)

"No, I'm sorry, Jessica. It's too close to supper time."

"But, Dad, I can go and be back in time."

"No, I'm sorry, Jessica. Supper is in fifteen minutes and you really don't have time."

"But I'll just be there real fast. You'll see."

"No, I'm sorry, Jessica."

"You don't like me playing with Mari, do you?"

In truth, Mari can at times get temperamental, and there have been instances where play was ended by one or the other parent because of fighting.

"I don't have any trouble with your playing with Mari."

"Yes, you do. You think she's too wild. I heard you say so to Mommy."

Not exactly, but he had said something similar.

"Sometimes the two of you can get pretty intense, but we like Mari."

"No, you don't. That's why you don't want me to go over there. You don't like any of my friends."

"Yes, I do, Jessica. That's ridiculous."

"No, it's not. You just want me home by myself all the time."

Jessica pulls in a completely new but provocative topic, hoping to divert her father from the original issue, which was letting her go out when supper was in fifteen minutes. This is not the time to get into that other issue about Mari. Stay on the subject:

"But, Dad, I can go and be back."

"No, I'm sorry, Jessica."

"You don't like me playing with Mari, do you?"

But Jessica's father does not want to touch it.

"No, Jessica. Supper will be in fifteen minutes."

"You hate Mari, don't you?"

Jessica's father should say no more.

"You do. You hate Mari. You hate all my friends. You know you do."

If Jessica's father feels that this is an issue that needs to be discussed, he might bring it up later.

"Do you really think we don't like Mari?"

"Sometimes I do. Yeah."

"No, we do like Mari. It's just that sometimes you two really butt heads. But that's okay. We like Mari. We like you and her being friends."

But he doesn't want to get into this now.

Another example of not-useful continuation:

"No, I'm sorry, Jason. We won't have time to go to Toys 'n' Stuff."

"But you never take me anywhere I want to go. You never do."

"You know that's not true. You get to go to plenty of places. Just last week we made that special trip to the Butterfly and Bug Museum just for you."

"No, it wasn't for me. I didn't want to go. I didn't like it."
"You said you did."
"I didn't. I hated it."
"Well, you said you liked it."
"Well, I didn't."

Better:

"No, Jason, I'm sorry we won't have time to go to Toys 'n' Stuff."
"But you never take me anywhere I want. You never do."
"I'm sorry. We won't have time."
"But I never get to go anywhere. I don't . . . I don't . . . I don't . . . I don't get to go anywhere . . . I don't . . . I don't."

Jason's mother says no more.

Disappointed Children

"No" creates a basic problem for children. They feel frustrated and disappointed, and they are not wrong to feel that way. But your early disengagement can actually help them get past their frustrations and disappointments and move on.

Four-year-old Juan and his family were getting into their car following a happy day at Uncle Danny's Wonder Fun World.

"Juan, you have to hold on to the balloon tighter or else it—"
"MY BALLOON!"
"Juan, I told you that—"
"MY BALLOON!"

And Juan's helium-filled balloon rose gracefully into the afternoon sky, shortly to become but a tiny dot against the gradually setting sun.

"MY BALLOON! MY BALLOON! I WANT ANOTHER BALLOON!"

"I'm sorry, Juan. That's it today for balloons."

"I WANT ANOTHER BALLOON!"

"No, I'm sorry, Juan. I know you feel bad about the balloon, but we can't go back in and get you another one."

"But I want another balloon. I want my balloon!"

"Well, I can't fly up and get it, Juan."

"Get me another balloon!"

"Maybe we can get one another time."

"No. I want a balloon now! Get me a balloon!"

"No, Juan, I'm sorry."

"I want a balloon! I want a balloon! You have to get me a balloon!"

Juan has lost his balloon and he's not going to get another one. He now has to deal with a real disappointment. In order to get over that disappointment and move on, Juan will have to go through a minor, but still quite real, grieving process for his lost balloon. He *will* be sad for a while—and then he *will* get over it.

Thanks to the nurturing that has already been laid down inside them and is part of them, children, except for those who have been seriously abused or neglected, have the capacity to work through the normal disappointments of day-to-day living all on their own. In fact, in order for them to grow and to mature, much of that work *must* be done by themselves.

But in order to do so they need practice. As long as their parents do not interfere and get in the way of the process, children have the means within their own little bodies to make the bad feelings go away in a relatively short time. All they have to do is wait a little while and gradually it happens.

Likewise, you need practice to learn that they can do this. You cannot always fill the rough spaces in your children's lives. Sometimes this means that you have to make decisions that will make your children unhappy, and you then have to watch them suffer. But if you don't, they won't learn to survive—at least for a while—without you.

As our children grow, we must leave space for them to learn to deal with whatever they encounter in their day-to-day lives. For deep traumas, serious upsets, or major disappointments, children need as much of our help as they can get. But for working through their bad feelings from the frustrations and disappointments of day-to-day living—toys they can't get, televisions they can't watch, potato chips that are too soggy— they need to be left on their own.

In the example with Juan, the more Juan's parents actively try to help him deal with his disappointment past a point early in the sequence, the more the baby self in Juan will latch on to his parents and get into the endless baby-self craving that can never be satisfied.

I can't get another balloon, so I'll fill up on Daddy.

The piggyness of the baby self strikes again. Rather than subsiding, fussing continues and may even increase. Hence, a better way:

"MY BALLOON! MY BALLOON!"
"I'm sorry, Juan. That's it today for balloons."
"I WANT ANOTHER BALLOON!"
"No, I'm sorry, Juan. I know you loved your balloon."
"I WANT ANOTHER BALLOON!"
"C'mon, honey. We have to get in the car and go home."
"I WANT ANOTHER BALLOON!"

But at that point, Juan's father should say no more about balloons. Perhaps he lifts his sobbing son into the car, perhaps he gives him some hugs. Then the family heads off.

"I want a balloon! I want a balloon! I want a balloon! I want a balloon!" sobs Juan in the backseat.

But with no further response from his father, Juan gradually will move on.

"I want a balloon. I want a balloon. I want a balloon."

But now Juan has found his Teddy, and after hugging it for a while, his interest turns to what is going on outside the car window.

"Why are trucks so big?"
"Because they carry lots of stuff."
"What stuff?"
"I don't know. Anything. Orange juice and furniture."

Juan has moved on and the balloon tragedy is now behind him.

Another example:

An enraged five-year-old Corey is screaming in his room. His mother deposited him there after he threw a major tantrum when she temporarily took a toy away from him because he was about to break it:

"You're not fair. I hate you. I do. I hate you," sobbed Corey.

But then if he is left alone in his room, with his anger and disappointment, a funny thing happens.

I hate Mommy. I do. I hate Mommy. She's not fair. She never is. I hate her. I wish I had a different mommy. Not her. She's mean. She doesn't care about me . . .

Nobody cares about me. Nobody does. Nothing ever happens to me that's good. Only bad . . .

Bad things don't happen to Billy Solomon. He gets everything he wants. He has a better bike than me. I wish I lived in his house . . .

No, I wish I lived in a palace. And I got everything, all for me. And I'd have a pet tiger. And he'd eat people I don't like. I wonder what tigers eat—besides people? I wonder if they eat cereal? I'm sort of hungry. But not for cereal. I wonder what's for supper.

"Mom, what's for supper?"

Not twenty minutes after a sobbing and furious Corey had been placed in his room, and with no intervention at all by his mother, he emerges in a totally good mood, as if nothing had happened.

To learn to deal with bad feelings on one's own is one of the foundations of mental health. Most children develop this skill. But some get stuck. Unable to deal with disappointment, they carry situations on and on and on, seeking resolutions they can never get, unable to take a loss and move on. Or, they become wholly dependent on others to deal with such feelings. You do want to be wary of being too helpful in resolving all of your children's bad feelings, especially where you are the ogre and your only crime is going against what they want. Sometimes they do need to learn that they can survive—at least for a while—without you.

5

What Comes after "No"

You have said "no." You've disengaged as quickly as possible and you're now facing a child who might be fussing, sulking, or gearing up for a temper tantrum. What should you do next? The answer: go about your business, continue the flow of your own life. Whatever you were doing, continue doing it, or move on to doing something else. You want to leave them behind with their baby selves.

Sulking

Perhaps no place is this idea of continuing the flow of your life, of not getting caught up in their angry snits, more clearly appropriate than when dealing with one of the baby self's favorite techniques—sulking.

BJ wanted to go to Burger Barn. Reenie wanted to go to Burgers Are Us. The family went to Burgers Are Us. Through out the ten-minute ride, BJ sat in the backseat of the car with a particularly grim look on his face and said nothing. Standing in line at Burgers Are Us, BJ's mother asked her son,

"What would you like BJ?"
Sulk

Confronted by a sulk, one does not want to *do* anything to get the sulker out of his or her sulking. With skilled sulkers, anything you do only plays into the sulk, as all parents know. Nothing you *do* works.

Not the frontal attack:

"I'm sick and tired of your acting like a baby about everything. Every time you don't get your way, you sulk. I'll give you something to sulk about."
This will only redouble the sulking.

Not jollying them:

"Come on BJ, sweetheart. It's not so bad. Let's see a little smile. Just a little one."
Sulkers love that one.

Not reasoning with them:

"I know you're mad. We'll go to Burger Barn another time. This time it's Reenie's turn."
This one might actually get somewhere, but usually not. BJ already knows it's Reenie's turn. It's just that the baby self wants all the turns.

Not a negative approach:

"Well, then I guess you don't want anything."
This is too much of a challenge to the sulker and will usually only increase the sulking.

The best response to sulking? Do nothing and allow it to run its course. BJ's parents should treat him as their beloved child who happens to be in a bad mood and is choosing not to talk. They should continue the flow of their lives in a happy upbeat manner. It then becomes BJ's choice whether he joins them or continues his sulk.

"What would you like, BJ?"
Sulk

"Well, I'll get you a Super Burger with cheese, fries, and a coke." This is BJ's mother's best guess as to what she thinks her son would want. "Is that okay? Let me know if you want something different."
Sulk

BJ's mother then orders, knowing that she gave him the chance to speak up if he wanted something different.

At the table, while BJ sits with the family but turns around in his seat looking away and ignoring his food, his mother starts a conversation with his sister:

"How do you like your sandwich, Reenie?"
"It's good. I like their fish sandwiches."
"My burger's okay, but they always put too much ketchup on for me."
"Why don't you scrape it off, Mommy?"
"No, it's not so bad. I'll just eat it as it is."

If they keep going while allowing BJ his sulk, sooner or later he will rejoin his family:

"Mine's okay, but I still like the Burger Deluxe at Burger Barn better."

This reconciliation will happen far sooner, and sulking will happen far less, if parents simply continue the flow of their lives with or without the participation of their sulking child. In effect you want to say to the sulker:

You can sulk as long as you want. It is totally okay with me. I'm not going to try to get you out of it, but I am not going to pay any special attention to you either. You may be in a bad mood, but I'm not. I'm going to continue being in my good mood. I'm going to go about my normal business, which includes loving you a lot.

Temper Tantrums

But what if their response to your "no" escalates to the point where going about your business is not so easy?

It was Saturday morning. Four-year-old Alex's father was taking dirty clothes out of Alex's room to put them in the wash.

"No, don't take my doggy shirt. I want to wear my doggy shirt."
"I'm sorry, Alex. It needs to be washed."
"But I want to wear my doggy shirt."
"I'm sorry, Alex. It needs washing and I'm doing the laundry this morning. You'll have to wear something else."

Alex's father then proceeded to carry the armful of dirty clothes out of Alex's room into the hallway in order to add them to the pile that was going to the Laundromat. Alex followed his father.

"Don't take my doggy shirt! I want to wear my doggy shirt!" Alex began trying to pull the doggy shirt out from the bundle that his father was carrying.

"No, Alex," said his father, lifting the clothes out of his son's reach. "You can't have the doggy shirt. It needs to be washed."

Alex then began tugging at his father, simultaneously screaming, "I want my doggy shirt! I want it!"
"No, Alex!"

Alex started to cry and began tugging even harder at his father.

"I want my doggy shirt! I want my doggy shirt!" Alex then threw himself on the floor, kicking and screaming. "I want it! I want it!"

When you think about it, the fact that a child is throwing a tantrum is not necessarily a bad sign at all. In fact, it is usually an indication that parents have done their job. They have appropriately set a limit—usually an unpopular one—and consequently frustrated their child, whose temper tantrum is a strong expression of displeasure. Temper tantrums are pure baby self.

Let's say Alex's father has definitely decided to stand firm. Alex will not get to wear the doggy shirt that morning. The first approach in the face of the ensuing tantrum should be sympathetic. Sulkers usually scorn positive offers in order to make those at whom they are mad suffer, but tantrum throwers may be open to simple nurturing.

"I know you're disappointed, honey. You really want to wear your doggy shirt today. And I know you're sad that you can't wear it. But you could wear it lots and lots of other times."

Sometimes this will be all that Alex needs.

"I did. I did. I wanted to wear my doggy shirt. I love my doggy shirt. I do. It's my favorite. Is my monster shirt clean?"

Or simple affection:

"Come here, honey. You want a hug?"

Which maybe Alex will accept, maybe suck his thumb a little, and then move on.

But often tantrum throwers are not so easily appeased, leading parents to try stronger tactics. Threats, for example:

"You better cut that out now or you're in big trouble."

Usually that will just get angrier responses.

"*You're* in big trouble!"

Or reasoning:

"Now, Alex, the temper tantrum is not going to get you anything. I'm not going to change my mind. You always have liked your fish shirt, and it's clean. You'll see, it will be just as much fun to wear."

Which might work, but more often you'll get this:

"I hate my fish shirt."
"But you've always said you liked your fish shirt."
"I don't. I hate it. I want my doggy shirt. I want it."

So what should you do if it looks like a tantrum is not going to go away? Once a tantrum has begun, it is a mistake to try to *do* something about it. You shouldn't *try* to end it. Instead you want to disengage, to back off. Beyond very early attempts to head off the tantrum, you only feed the baby self, regardless of your response. Tantrums feed off any kind of parental response. The swifter that a tantrum thrower is left on his own to deal with his disappointment at not getting his way, the sooner the tantrum will wind down. You don't want to get in the way of that process, so you simply continue to go about your own business, as hard as that may be.

"I want my doggy shirt. I want my doggy shirt," sobs Alex, still lying on the floor, kicking and screaming.
"If you want me, I'll be hunting for change for the Laundromat."
"I want my doggy shirt," continues to sob Alex.

But Alex's father is no longer interested as he goes about their apartment hunting for change.

"I want my doggy shirt," calls out Alex.

But nobody seems to be listening.

"I do. I want my doggy shirt."

Gradually, if Alex's father remains oblivious to the tantrum, Alex will drop it, and the temper tantrum will be

over far more quickly than if his father had intervened at
length.

"Can I put the money in at the Laundromat?"
"Of course, Alex."

Tantrums can be very unpleasant to be around and sometimes too awful to ignore. You do not want to ignore a tantrum that is getting under your skin, because you're not really
ignoring it. You're *trying* to ignore it, but without success.
Invariably what will happen is your irritation will build to a
point where you explode. You end up giving the baby self a
big emotional serving of your attention, which is exactly what
it is after and exactly what you don't want to give it.

So if you *start* to get irritated—separate, and I mean *separate*. Very young tantrum throwers are immediately banished
until the tantrum is over. With young tantrum throwers like
Alex, this often may mean picking them up and carrying them
to their rooms. If they don't stay, you put them back—which
sometimes may mean multiple swift trips back and forth to
their rooms. (We'll talk in the next chapter about what to do
with older kids who are too big to carry.) If a parent does this
quickly and regularly, children will eventually go on their
own, knowing that if they do not they *will* be carried, and if
they do not stay, they will be carried back again. It's a good
message. If a temper tantrum is too unpleasant to ignore, separation will be an early and inevitable result, whether volun-
tarily or involuntarily.

But the tantrum thrower is welcome back once the
tantrum subsides, even if the improvement is instantaneous.

"I'll be good. I'll be good."

Fine. And if the tantrum truly has ended they're welcome
to stay. But should they return and start up the fussing again,

they are once more banished until the tantrum is over. Sometimes, if they are tired and in a really bad mood, this may take a substantial period of time. I prefer this approach to "time out," in which a child is banished for a specific amount of time and often to a specific punishment place. Separation does not need to be a *punishment*. Separation is a simple statement of fact.

You can have your tantrum, just not around me. As soon as you're ready to be pleasant again, you're welcome back.

This attitude teaches children that their tantrums inevitably and swiftly cause separation from you, which is just the opposite of what they want. It teaches them that their tantrums will get them nothing to feed on.

Out in Public

All of what I've just said works great when you are at home, but baby selves don't care where their temper tantrums take place.

"I want the yellow fluffy chicky."
"No, I'm sorry, Greta, we're not buying anything today."
"But I want the yellow fluffy chicky."
"No, Greta. No toys today."
"But I want the chicky."

As her mother stood in the checkout line of Leo's Home World, waiting to pay for a bath mat, five-year-old Greta, who had been fondly admiring the nearby Easter display of little stuffed chickies, started having a tantrum.

"I want a chicky! I want a chicky! I WANT A CHICKY!"

Meanwhile, all eyes in the rather long checkout line started to roll, tongues clucked, and heads shook at the scene of the mother and her obviously spoiled, out-of-control daughter. The whole line was thinking:

Can't you do something with that child. Buy her the stupid chicky, smack her. Anything. But shut her up. They shouldn't let mothers and kids like that in the store.

What to do?

"Actually, I'm not her mother. I'm her distant auntie who has her for a day. No, actually, I just found her. Would you like her?"

Well, I don't want to buy her the stupid chicky. She'll forget about it ten minutes after we leave the store, and I've already said "no." I don't want her to think her tantrums can help her get her way.

"I WANT A CHICKY! I WANT A CHICKY!"

This is a famously tough situation, because what is best for you and your child puts you in direct conflict with the wishes of everybody around you.

SHUT HER UP!

But what are the options?

Should you grab her, look her in the eye, and say in your meanest possible voice, "You just better be quiet?"

That might work for thirty seconds, after which the tantrum will resume with more energy.

Should you buy her the chicky, capitulating to all the angry onlookers?

That one would be a disaster, obviously, because it says quite clearly to Greta, "Your tantrums work. Keep them up."

Should you threaten her? "If you don't be quiet now, do not expect to go over to Kimberly's this afternoon."

Because baby selves only care about now, such threats, even if carried out later, are rarely useful in stopping the ongoing tantrum or in preventing future ones. Worse, the carried-out threats subsequently stick you with a whole other later scene when Greta is not allowed to go over to Kimberly's.

Should you go home?

Everybody in the store is rooting for this one. But going home is a particularly bad option. It inconveniences you because you had errands to complete. Worse, it gives too much power to the tantrum thrower. If she doesn't like what's going on, she can make you go home.

Should you divert her attention?

"I've got an idea. Let's see if there's anything interesting in my purse."

Fine, if it works, but chances are slim that it will. Besides, you don't always want to rely on diversions. Somewhere, somehow, she's going to have to learn to deal with disappointment.

So what do you do? Best by far is to tough it out, not giving in and not responding. *Regardless* of where a tantrum
takes place, the less it succeeds at getting you to change your
mind, the less it succeeds at getting any kind of a response,
the shorter it will be and the less likely it is that you will have
to endure another one. If you want to limit public tantrums,
you have to ride them out. You have to endure the looks,
maybe even the comments.

*Some people really shouldn't be allowed to have children.
It's a disgrace.*

Now, there are situations where parents should not subject others to a child having a tantrum: in a house of worship,
at a movie, in a fancy restaurant. But otherwise, public places
are public places, and the fact that people are occasionally
subjected to tantruming children comes with living in the
world.

It comes down to you against the rest of the world. They
want you to do something, *anything*, to shut up your kid. But
you need to do what is best for you, your child, and your future public outings, not what everybody around you wants
you to do. You can cave into pressure, but if you do, you will
pay. You have a tough choice.

"That's it, Greta. Since you can't behave, we're leaving."
"Yaay!" Spontaneous applause. "Yaay! Way to go. Good
choice. Bye, Greta."

Overall, what a parent wants to do about tantrums is
"nothing."

You can have tantrums, but they are not going to accomplish anything. Not only will I not change my mind, but your tantrum will get less, not more, of me.

If tantrums are continually rendered ineffective, they will be resorted to less, and their overall frequency, intensity, and duration will definitely be reduced. However, tantrums will not disappear altogether, because they are too much a part of being a child.

If They Hit

"No, Jeanine, I don't want you going into the kitchen drawers," said Jeanine's mother, closing the drawer that her five-year-old daughter had opened. Whereupon Jeanine turned and hit her mother on the back. Sometimes children hit, or kick, or pinch. This is not okay. You must always intervene. The line between angry words and physical aggression is a very important one.

Having been hit, Jeanine's mother must immediately turn to her daughter, hold her by the shoulders and say in a firm, very serious voice:

"No, you cannot hit me, Jeanine."

If Jeanine should continue hitting, her mother must hold her in such a way that Jeanine cannot hit her.

"No, Jeanine. I am not going to let you hit me."

But as soon as Jeanine stops hitting, Jeanine's mother must then let her go in order to allow her to continue her fussing. And every time hitting has occurred, regardless of how quickly it stopped, a parent should later, at a neutral time, say to the child:

"Today when you got mad, you hit me. It is okay to get mad at me. But you may not hit me."

Hitting is a serious provocation, but other consequences, including punishments, are not good. They only tend to make a child mad and subtract from the basic message that hitting is not okay. Longer discussions are also probably a mistake, because they deflect from your main leverage, which is your *very* strong disapproval.

The steps I recommend here may or may not work immediately. That is, episodes of hitting may continue, in which case the exact same procedure should be followed. But in the long run this procedure *will* work, and it will work more swiftly—for any given child—and with fewer other problems than anything else a parent might do. The hitting will stop. But hitting must be addressed—everytime.

Love and Understanding

Sometimes all that a frustrated, unhappy child may need is a little love and understanding. This is always a good place to start.

"I want to feed the goldfish," said four-year-old Natalie to her father.

"I'm sorry, Natalie, but they've already been fed, and it's not good for them if we give them too much food."

"But I want to feed the goldfish."

"I'm sorry, honey, you can feed them tomorrow. I'll make sure."

"But I want to feed the goldfish today."

"I'm sorry, honey."

"But I want to do it today. I want to feed the goldfish. I want to feed them today."

At that point, who knows why, maybe because she was tired, Natalie showed all the signs all too recognizable to her father of the start of a full-fledged tantrum.

"Here, honey. Let me give you a hug."

And Natalie, face sqinched up in extreme displeasure, nonetheless walked over to her father, who picked her up and gave her a long hug, during which time Natalie simply flopped like a rag doll on his shoulders. At the end of the hug, Natalie's father put her down and Natalie wandered off to check out toys on her toy shelf. The goldfish were forgotten.

"I don't see why I have to clear the table and do the dishes and Gracie doesn't have to do anything."
"Ivan, you know Gracie is still sick."
"She doesn't look sick to me. She could do it if she wanted to. She's such a faker. I'm not going to do everything just because Gracie, the faker, acts sick."
"I know you feel it's not fair when all the work falls to you. And you're right. I'm sure even though Gracie's sick, she's happy she doesn't have to do any chores."
"The faker."
"Well, I'd be mad too if I had to do everything just because I had a sick sister."
"I am mad. It's not fair. I'm going to get sick for a month and Gracie the faker will have to do everything. See how she likes it."

But then with minor grumbling, Ivan went off, cleared the table, and did the dishes.

But sometimes the love and understanding are not enough to help them through their disappointment, because the baby self simply wants more.

"Come here, Natalie, honey. Let me give you a hug."

"I don't want a hug. I want to feed the goldfish."

"I'll give you a *really* big hug."

"I don't want stupid hugs. I want to feed the goldfish. Why can't I? Why? I want to. I want to. I want to."

Or:

"I'm not going to do everything just because Gracie, the faker, acts sick."

"I know you feel it's not fair when all the work falls to you. And you're right. I'm sure even though Gracie's sick, she's happy she doesn't have to do any chores."

"That's right, it's not fair. Gracie's a stupid faker. I'm not going to do her job. I'm not going to do my job. Gracie's a faker."

"I know you feel mad."

"I'm not doing any jobs. I don't care what you say. You can't make me. You're unfair and you know it. Gracie gets everything. You love her better. You do."

If what you have offered seems unsatisfactory and they want more, you only have one option: disengage and, as always, make it fast.

Say It Later

"I did not like the way you behaved this afternoon. It made the whole afternoon unpleasant for everybody."

In many of the situations I've addressed up to this point, I have included the option of returning to an issue at a neutral time instead of during the confrontation itself. I suggested that Vinnie's mother might want to talk to him at a later time about his calling her a fat jerk and that Jessica's father might want to talk to her at a later time about her accusation that her parents don't like her friend Mari. I am briefly bringing this point up again, because it is an important tactic in successfully dealing with problem behavior.

Let me reiterate. Anything you say at the time of confrontation will just be used as a takeoff point for further arguing. It's just catnip for the baby self. If you feel that something needs to be said about your child's behavior, say it later at a neutral time, rather than at the time of confrontation. It is only later that your message will be heard, only then that it will have any true impact.

6

❖

"Stop"

How to Make Them

Firm decisions and swift disengagement are key when you're saying "no" to something that they want. But when kids are already in the middle of doing something that you want them to stop doing, your method of intervening needs to be a little different.

It is here that parents have traditionally relied on threats and punishments. But it is here that parents' special power over their children comes into play. In the scenarios that follow—except where physical intervention is necessary—what I describe works, and it works without recourse to threats and punishments. It works because, as a part of normal child development, children form a strong love attachment to their parents. Their parents become a part of them. Because of this love attachment, parents actually sit inside their child's head as permanent residents. And because of this, parents have enormous power over their child's feelings. As a result, when parents are emotionally distant, their child wants them back, and when parents are displeased, their child feels bad and wants the parents to stop being mad. They can't help it.

They say, "I don't care." But children *do* care. They always care. Most parents simply do not realize the power that this leverage gives them. They feel they must bring in other means, establish even more leverage, usually threats and punishment. They never witness their own *inherent* power because they never give it a chance.

Children hate it when a parent withdraws into a state of silent disapproval. Think of what it feels like in an adult love relationship, perhaps following an argument, when one of the partners is silently mad at the other.

Is she still mad at me?

"Lucy, I'm going out to get milk. I'll be back in about twenty minutes."
"Whatever."

Damn! She's still mad.

It is a very real power that we have over our children.

When They Are Little

When they are little and you want them to stop doing something, you need to intervene physically. That is, you need to go to them and physically prevent them from continuing what they are doing. Words are not to be relied upon.

"Matthew, please do not squirt the ketchup bottle."

Matthew is two and a half. If he does not stop, you immediately have to go over and take away the ketchup bottle. With the very young, actual physical intervention is your number one control. Words should accompany the interventions, but words alone don't work.

"No. Squirting the ketchup makes too much of a mess."

Explanations are good. Maybe they will understand, maybe they won't. Explanations are mainly investments for a future time when children can comprehend, internalize, and actually use the reasons you give as restraints on their own behavior. But at young ages, actual physical intervention must be the bottom line.

"Trisha, stop pulling at the curtain . . . Trisha, I said stop pulling at the curtain . . . Trisha, stop pulling at the curtain now . . . Trisha, do you hear me? . . . Trisha, I have had it with you. When are you going to listen?"

Why do I always have to tell her four times before she listens to me?

If you have to tell them four times, it's your fault, not theirs, because you should have acted sooner. If they do not obey, either act fast or don't do anything at all. In some situations, maybe you just don't feel like doing anything, because it's more trouble than it's worth, or you just don't care that much.

She's not really going to hurt the curtains, she's not strong enough to pull them down. I don't like her getting in the habit of doing it . . . but I don't really feel like getting up.

There's nothing wrong with this attitude. In fact, it teaches children at a very young age that there are two standards of obedience. They learn to differentiate the voice that means Daddy will swiftly get up and come over and stop me from the voice that means he's not going to do anything so I think I'll continue.

What about situations where a child's safety is at risk, like running out in the street or playing with kitchen chemicals that could be harmful? Again, you do not want to rely on your words as a control. If you are concerned about your child's safety, prevention, not obedience, takes precedence: you don't allow them to play near a street and you put any dangerous chemicals out of reach. When safety is an issue with very young children, it is your job, not theirs, to make sure that no serious harm can come to them.

As They Get Older

As children get older, direct physical intervention becomes less of an option. They get faster, bigger, and stronger.

"Timothy, please stop banging your fork on the table."

Since nine-year-old Timothy did not stop immediately, his father grabbed for the fork. But Timothy swiftly pulled away, whereupon his father made another reach for the fork. This time Timothy's father got hold of the fork, but because Timothy had wisely switched to holding the fork by its fat end, his father was only able to grab the smooth handle and had much less of a grip than his son. A struggle ensued, which was finally won by Timothy's father, but not before Timothy had sworn at his father and had jumped up from the table, glaring angrily.

"Don't you swear at me, Timothy."
"I wasn't hurting anything. I wasn't," a now-very-angry Timothy yells at his father.

Once children get big enough to create a significant struggle, physical intervention is no longer a viable option. The struggle, regardless of outcome, becomes too stimulating in and of itself, and absolutely works against you. It will only extend the battle and produce more, not less, of the same in the future. Your best option when older children do not immediately comply is to repeat the request in a matter-of-fact manner and *stay there and wait*. Respond to nothing further that they do or say until they comply.

Your basic stance as you wait for them to comply should be the same as your attitude while waiting for a bus.

I am here.
I am waiting.
I expect you to stop.
I am not enjoying the wait.
I am not going anywhere until you do what I have asked.

Which translates into:

"Timothy, please stop banging your fork on the table."

"It's not hurting anything," says Timothy, continuing his banging.

"Timothy, please stop banging your fork." And then Timothy's father swiftly withdraws into a waiting silence.

"It's *not* hurting anything," grumbles Timothy.

Almost certainly, Timothy will then comply, but not immediately, not without a brief "you can't boss me around" pause—you have to live with this. Once he does comply—and he will, the vast majority of the time—"Thank you" is almost always the best response. Definitely not, "Why do you always have to give me a hard time when I ask you to do anything?" At best this accomplishes nothing, and at worst it opens up a new argument. Parents should avoid all such cans of worms.

But what if they don't stop? As mentioned, if it is possible to intervene physically without getting into a major battle, that is the first option—it is the only option if what they are doing is potentially dangerous. Otherwise, if they persist, the best strategy is to do as just described: make the demand and wait—and do not get into a verbal battle. With real children in real situations, in order to achieve compliance as swiftly as possible this *is* what works best.

Later—not then—if the persistent noncompliance was something you feel needs to be addressed, you can bring it up.

"I asked you not to make all that noise while your little sister was napping, but you kept shouting anyway and woke her up. I did not like what you did."

Last, as will be discussed shortly, there are many situations where, if you believe that persistent noncompliance may occur in the future, this can be prevented by temporarily removing the means by which it would.

This procedure applies also to older children, who are too big to be carried easily elsewhere, are banished but refuse to leave. Parents should repeat what they have to say and then wait.

After supper nine-year-old Tyrone had wanted to make freezer pops, but his father said "no," since he was in the middle of cleaning up the kitchen. Tyrone, however, persisted with his request. His father stood firm.

"No, I'm sorry, Tyrone, another time but not tonight."

At that point Tyrone launched into a full-fledged fuss with no indication of letting up.

"You never let me do anything, you never do. I never get to do anything."

"Good-bye, Tyrone," said his father.

Tyrone, making no move to leave, remained in the kitchen, glaring belligerently at his father.

"I'm not going. You can't make me. I'm not."

Tyrone's father says nothing.

"I'm not. I'm not going."

But Tyrone is now talking to himself. Further, he has a real problem. His father's request for him to leave and his father's standing disapproval are both now in Tyrone's head, and both make him feel uncomfortable. And he has no way to get rid of this feeling.

"I am *not* going." And Tyrone kicks at a table leg, desperately hoping to reengage his father. "I'm not."

Unfortunately for Tyrone, it's not possible to stay in the room, maintain his disobedience, and still be relaxed. His father's silent disapproval sits too uncomfortably in his head to allow this. Were Tyrone able to draw his father back into his fussing, he then would not have to keep the bad feelings inside himself. He could vent them onto his father. But now he has to struggle with the bad feelings on his own.

"You're not fair. You're never fair. You're not."

Tyrone, with one last kick at the table leg, exits.

The stance described here is not always easy, but if you can do it, it works well and surprisingly swiftly.

When children know that your expectation that they comply will not go away, that you will remain, waiting, but that their noncompliance cannot pull you into a fight, long episodes of noncompliance will greatly decrease—though, as with temper tantrums, not totally disappear.

Removing the Means of Misbehavior

As mentioned, there is another option for the times when they persist in doing what you do not want them to do. This is where future misbehavior can be prevented by removing the means of doing it.

Kenneth is allowed to play video games one hour each day. That's it. But when his mother tells him to stop, he regularly keeps on playing, only stopping after a considerable amount of fuss. Here Kenneth's mother has an easy option. She can suspend video game play for the next few days.

We will allow you to play video games. But only if you do it following our rules.

Kenneth's mother will restore the video game playing. She will renew that opportunity. But if the privilege is again abused, the result will be the same.

A parent can continue this indefinitely.

You can play video games for an hour. But if you give me a hard time about it, you won't be playing for the next few days.

Or a bicycle is temporarily taken away when Kenneth goes outside the geographic limits that are clearly understood, Magic Markers are taken away to prevent his writing on walls, a hard rubber ball is temporarily taken away when he throws it against walls inside the house, or a very nice fishing knife is temporarily confiscated when he throws it at a tree too near his siblings.

In all of these situations, a direct consequence of the bad behavior is an unpleasant result. But it is not a punishment because the intent is not to cause suffering but rather to temporarily eliminate the possibility of the forbidden behavior occurring.

When They've Done Wrong

But what about when they've already done something they knew they weren't supposed to?

"Isabel," said her father to his seven-year-old daughter. "There's a box of cupcakes on the counter. Please do not eat any of them. I need them all for my bridge club tonight. Do you understand?"

"Yes," said Isabel, but an hour later her father happened to look into the kitchen and saw Isabel finishing off what turned out to be her second cupcake. Isabel's father was now confronted with the fact that his daughter had disobeyed him. She had committed a crime. Obviously not a very big one, but clearly a crime. What should he do?

What Isabel's father should do is confront his daughter and in a serious voice say to her:

"Isabel, I asked you not to eat any of the cupcakes but you did. Now I am not going to have enough cupcakes for this evening. I specifically asked you not to but you did."

That's it?!

Yes. That's it. This simple statement is the best possible response to his daughter's crime.

But there have to be consequences. Isabel absolutely did what she was not supposed to do. How will she ever learn not to do bad things again?

First, there definitely were consequences. Isabel's father was seriously displeased with what his daughter had done, and he communicated this displeasure to his daughter.

That's not going to do anything.

In real life, with real children—because of the inevitable love attachment of child to parent—what actually would happen following Isabel's father's statement would be that Isabel would immediately get upset and either cry; get defensive and say, "I didn't hear you, I didn't"; or get angry, as a counteroffensive and as an attempt to dispel the bad feelings she is experiencing.

"It's not fair. We never have cupcakes. Only for your stupid meetings."

Regardless of her response, Isabel would feel bad. If her father then says no more, Isabel can't deflect her bad feelings onto him. Her unpleasant, *guilty* feelings sit inside of her.

"It's all your fault. It is. I *never* get cupcakes. That's why I had to take them."

If Isabel's father now stays clear, she is stuck having to swallow the bad feelings all on her own. She will feel bad for a while, but the bad feelings eventually will go away.

"Are you mad at me, Daddy?"
"No, but I wish you hadn't eaten the cupcakes."
"I'm sorry. I won't do it again."

The next time Isabel is confronted by a similar choice, the memory of her father's displeasure and the problem it caused for him—and therefore for her—will come into her head, and it will be a significant force against her repeating her crime. Maybe the temptation will still be too great and she will do it again, but the memory will still have very real preventive power.

Why do it this way? Because over time, as Isabel matures, this is the best possible way to produce a real conscience, a conscience not based on the fear of what will happen to oneself, but on the fear of possible harm to others.

Even if I don't get caught, it will upset Daddy because he won't have enough cupcakes for his meeting.

Even the best consciences do not always control our behavior. But good consciences weigh not just the potential pain to oneself but the potential for suffering of others.

Moral Teaching

There are very real rights and wrongs. How do we teach them to our children?

Samantha's mother was tired, having had a long day.

"Samantha, would you help me bring in some of the groceries from the car?"

"I can't. I'm too tired," whined Samantha, who wasn't tired at all but just didn't feel like carrying in any groceries, and who promptly flopped down on the couch, refusing to budge. "I'm so tired."

Samantha's mother, forced to bring in the groceries by herself, responded angrily:

"Samantha, I did not appreciate that. I've had a hard day and I needed your help. You were very selfish."

Samantha, feeling guilty but also refusing to concede an inch, whined, "I'm just so tired. I *am* tired. I'm just so tired. You don't believe me. But I am. I think I'm sick."

"I did not like that," said her mother, her tone reflecting her anger as she turned and left the room.

Samantha lay on the couch for maybe ten minutes, seeing if she could pick out animal shapes in the bare branches outside the window. But then, growing bored, she thought of a drawing set that she had gotten as a present, hadn't played with in a while, and that she knew was now on a high shelf in the closet, too high for her to get on her own.

"Mom, could you get down for me my drawing set that's on the shelf in the closet?"

Having put away the groceries, Samantha's mother was now resting and still did feel some residual irritation about her daughter's earlier selfish laziness. Nonetheless she said,

"Okay, Samantha," got up and went to the closet and pulled down the drawing set for her daughter.

"Thank you, Mommy."

Moral lesson to Samantha: *It is better that one be nice to others, even when they have acted toward you like a spoiled brat.*

The reverse, a tit-for-tat retaliation, would be a normal and understandable reaction, but it would have taught a very different lesson.

"No, Samantha, I'm not in the mood to do you any favors after you didn't help me. Maybe next time you'll think before you are lazy and selfish."

That moral lesson to Samantha: *If people do not do for you, you shouldn't do for them.*

Obviously, not all parents are going to respond as did Samantha's mother. But the two different underlying moral lessons are there. *Do unto others as you would have others do unto you.* Or, *An eye for an eye, a tooth for a tooth.*

How we act toward our kids and how they see us deal with others when a wrong has been done is the single strongest source of moral teaching that we parents have.

But what about when they truly have done wrong? Shouldn't they be taught lessons about that? Obviously, the answer is "yes."

"Kelvin, Mrs. Forrester called today and told me that you and a couple of other kids had been teasing Kendra Porcello and that the teasing was very mean."

"I didn't. It wasn't me. It was Michael and Garth."

Kelvin's mother's information was that her son definitely actively participated in the teasing, and she believed her source. Not picking up on his denials, she continued:

"Mean teasing like that is very wrong. Kendra can't defend herself and I feel very sorry for her. What you did was very bad. I know the other kids tease. But it is very wrong. I really hope that you won't do it again."

In the face of real wrongs, you need to confront your child as strongly and as seriously as you can, expressing your real *feelings* about what he did. Here your emotions *are* appropriate. You want to get across in no uncertain terms how you feel about the wrongdoing. Because of your son's attachment to you, he will hear it.

Teasing is something that Mommy feels is very bad.

Children will feel bad. They will feel guilty. Guilty enough that they will never do it again? Maybe yes, maybe no. But this is your most powerful response. When children have done wrong, punishment is always tempting, but punishment will only get in the way of good moral teaching. The message that you want them to get is:

My parent, whom I love and who is a part of me, feels that what I did was wrong.

But the message of punishment is:

What I did will cause bad things to happen to me (if I get caught).

The basic problem with punishment for teaching what is good and bad is that intentionally causing suffering—which is what punishment is—is a basic part of the lesson. If punishment were necessary in order to raise civilized children—as the only means of teaching good and bad—then we would be stuck with it. But it is not. Because of children's automatic love attachment to their parents, parents fully have the power to do the job just by communicating to their children what they believe. Punishment is not necessary.

Further, children raised under a system that does without the intentional infliction of suffering will themselves be less likely to cause suffering to others.

Again, for teaching moral lessons, the strongest tool that you have is how you genuinely feel.

7

"Do"
How to Make Them Do
What They Don't Feel
Like Doing

"Gregory, would you please hang up your wet towel?"

"I can't. I'm already in bed. I'll do it tomorrow."

"You're not already in bed. You're not even nearly in bed. Please hang up the towel, now."

"But I'm getting ready for bed. And besides I'm too tired. I'm really tired. I said I'll do it tomorrow."

"Gregory, hang up the towel."

"I said I would do it tomorrow." Still dressed, Gregory jumps into bed. "I really am in bed now. I can't do it."

How do you make children do things that they do not feel like doing? Picking up after themselves. Brushing their teeth. Helping with the dishes. The truth is that this is probably the most difficult piece of parenting with today's kids. Doing what they don't feel like doing is not a natural behavior of children when left to their own devices.

Hmm. I can't decide which I'll do first. Pick up my room, take out the trash, or vacuum the living room? Choices. Choices.

It turns out that parents who get kids to do what they don't feel like doing have two basic things in common. Let's look at several families as examples. One family I knew particularly impressed me. They were a nice family, and, as far as I could tell, not so different from other families—with one very notable exception. All of the children in the family did housework with no fussing. They just did it. I was so impressed that on a couple of occasions I talked with the mother of the family, who generously answered my questions about the secret to their success.

The key point I took away from these interrogations was the importance of her and her husband's *expectations* of their children. That the children would do the requested tasks was what she called a "given." There was no discussion, no leeway, no possibility of argument. Also, she said she and her husband never used rewards or punishment.

My wife, Mary Alice, and I wanted our children, Nick and Margaret, to learn to play a musical instrument. They both took piano lessons, but neither stayed with it very long, although we encouraged them not to quit. As a child, I had a baby self and a half, and I lasted all of one piano lesson. But I wanted my kids to do better. "You will regret quitting once you are older. I know I did." I would often say this—to no avail. Meanwhile, a couple we knew had four children, all of whom became accomplished musicians. How did they succeed where we failed? How did those parents get all four of their kids to keep playing? Yes, they were musically inclined, and music appreciation ran in the family. Yes, being a musician was given a special respect within the family. But mainly those parents put a lot of time and energy into getting their kids to stay with it. Few people are born loving to practice an instrument. Those parents really persisted, far more than Mary Alice and I did. We cared. We persisted. But not enough.

What to Do

These two stories illustrate two basic facts about getting kids to do what they don't feel like doing.

One is that the one true, effective leverage is the absolute expectation that a task must be done and there is no other choice. The ultimate leverage is *not* what will happen if they don't do what is asked. The ultimate leverage is not "or else." It is not negative consequences. The ultimate leverage is that there is no alternative. The demand and expectation are unremitting; neither will go away until the task is done.

The second fact is that, at least initially, there has to be considerable time and effort put in by the parents. You have to be there until the task is done. And you have to be there again and again each time the task arises.

Rewards, not harsh punishments, consequences, and motivational talks are fine. They all work at first. But in the long run, over the course of a childhood, they do not hold up. Absolute and unremitting expectation and parental presence are the only way.

Lydia's mother makes her request:

"Lydia, now that you're finished playing with your Tiny Trucks, please put them away. Otherwise they're going to get stepped on."

"No, they won't. They won't get stepped on."

Then if Lydia does not do it right away, her mother needs to repeat the request and wait.

"Lydia, please put away the trucks."
"Why do I always have to pick up stuff? They're okay where they are."
"Lydia, they need to be picked up now."
"No, they don't. They're okay."

At this point Lydia's mother should say no more. She remains present; that is all. She hasn't picked up on any of her daughter's arguments. The request, clearly stated and restated, remains in force. What Lydia's mother now needs to do is wait. Her attitude as she waits is relaxed but also immovable. In effect:

I expect you to do it. I can't make you do it, and I'm not going to try. But it needs to be done, and I have no plans to go anywhere until that happens. I can't make you do it, but it must be done.

Imagine you need to get inside your house but the door is locked and your child, who is the only one who can let you in, is on the other side of that door. But your child, for whatever reason, refuses to open the door. You're not going anywhere. You can't *make* her do it. But it has to happen—there is no alternative. And until it does happen, you and the absolute expectation remain.

With the vast majority of kids, this procedure will work the vast majority of the time. Lydia will comply.

Perhaps gracefully:

"There, Mommy. I'm doing good, aren't I?"

Or perhaps not so gracefully:

"I always have to pick things up. I'm so tired."

Either way is okay.

"Thank you, Lydia."

Definitely no negative comments:

"I wish sometimes you could surprise me by doing something as soon as I ask."

Not only thank them, but when they do the task regularly recognize their efforts.

"Thank you, Lydia. It is a big help to me that you have been picking up your toys."

It makes a big difference to kids. If they receive no recognition:

What's the point. They don't even notice it when I do it.

When recognized:

I'm helping. Mom likes it.

Kids do think this way.

Finally, if you want children to learn to do a particular task on a regular basis, if you want that task to become a *habit*, the only way to make it a habit is to continue regularly to make that demand.

"Lydia, did you remember to pick up your toys when you were done with them?"

"Sort of."

"Please go in and pick them up."

If you do not repeat requests, kids who have faithfully been doing the tasks will often slack off. Rightly or wrongly they do assume:

Oh, I guess it's okay now not to do it anymore because Mom hasn't said anything about it in a while.

The ever present baby self will always look for an out.

I'll Do It Later

"Later" does not work.

"Jimmy, please put away the glasses from the dish drain."

"I will. Later."

The problem with later is that later rarely happens. Instead, you have to start all over again, but at this point you're probably a little angry at having to repeat your request.

"Jimmy, I thought you said you were going to take care of the glasses. Why can't you simply do what I ask and get it over with?"

"I will. Later."

Much better, from the start:

"No, Jimmy, I need the glasses to be put away now."
"But I'll do it later. I promise."
"No, Jimmy, please do it now."

The one exception is when the task does not need to be done immediately and a child is legitimately in the middle of an activity—a TV show they like and always watch, a game where pausing is difficult. But if you allow for this kind of exception, you must accept that you more than likely will need to repeat the request later.

"I thought you said you were going to hang up the towel when your game was over."
"Oh yeah. Well, I can't do it now because I'm in the middle of another game. I'll do it later. I promise."
"No, Justin, this time you have to do it now."
"But my game!"
"Now, Justin!"

The Towel

Jason, you need to hang up your towel.
I can't. I'm busy. I'll do it later. I'm tired.
No, Jason, I need you to hang up your towel now.
But I can't. I'm tired. I said I'll do it later. Why do you always pick on me?
No, Jason. I need it done now.
But I can't. I'm tired. I'm sick. Why can't you do it? You're mean. Why does it have to be done now?

I Forgot

"Did you feed Mr. Spooky like you were supposed to?"
"I forgot."
"Well, maybe I'll just forget to buy and cook food for a month. What do you think of that?"
"We could go to McDonald's."

Eventually they learn. But if it is totally left up to them, tasks to be done have an amazing ability to slip right out of their short-term memory storage and into the great void.

Difficult Tasks

Some jobs are truly difficult, especially for younger children. They may balk at doing them, not so much out of laziness or stubbornness, but because to them the task seems truly overwhelming. Examples of this might be a gigantic toy mess, or, with younger kids, making the bed in the morning. Here, a good strategy is to begin the task without them, but request that they participate.

"Come on, Jannelle, your toys need to be picked up."
"But I can't. I'm too tired."
"Jannelle, they need to be put away. I'm going to start working on it, but I need you to help me."

And, usually, if her mother persists:

"Come on, Jannelle, I do need your help."
"Oh, okay. What should I do?"

Direct Defiance

What if a child flat out refuses to do what is asked? What happens, what does it mean, what should you do? This is an important issue that touches a very deep place inside all children—in fact, inside all of us. To answer, let me describe a common early-childhood phenomenon.

At some point most toddlers try the following experiment. Their parent says "Come here" and they say "no." The toddlers then watch to see whose orders their bodies will obey. They discover that their bodies obey them, not their parents. Usually, children find this discovery quite exciting, and they often repeat this game every chance they get, because it is so delightful to them. Their parents find it somewhat less delightful.

"Raphael, come here," says Raphael's father to his two-year-old son.

"No," and Raphael runs off in the other direction, squealing with delight.

Prior to the experiment, Raphael really didn't know what would happen, didn't know whose will actually controls his body. Children are very pleased to see that it is they alone who rule their bodies. Parents can move them around from the outside, but only they can cause their bodies to act. This matter of *will*, of who is in charge of our body, is terribly important to us. By nature, starting in early childhood, we care intensely that we are the ultimate boss of our own bodies. Children need to establish that they are this boss. Having established that fact, most of the time they are content. But sometimes they just need to reaffirm it. Hence, Zachary and his father:

"Zachary, would you please pick up your crayons?"

"I won't and you can't make me." *(Just in case you forgot, I am the boss of me.)*

We want to respect this. If our children, for no apparent reason, absolutely refuse to do something that we want them to do, we do not want to pull out our big guns to get them in line. We can let them know that we still want them to do it, that we expect them to do it, that we are displeased that they are not doing it, that we will continue to expect that they will do it in the future. But we do not want to try to force them with big punishments, or to get or stay very angry over a long period of time in order to *make* them obey.

"Zachary, if you do not pick up those crayons you're going to get in big trouble."

No. Not big trouble. We want to say that, if they absolutely refuse, they definitely risk our displeasure, but nothing truly terrible will happen. Problems arise only when parents cannot accept that their children might occasionally defy them. If parents do not truly respect their children's absolute right to be the boss of themselves, then it will become an ongoing issue, because children will never let it pass. It turns into a battle of wills.

"Okay, Zachary, you're in your room and you are not coming out until you pick up the crayons. And I mean it."

The danger is that since Zachary's right as the undisputed ruler of his own body is now seriously challenged, every request can set up a need for another declaration of independence. Or the field of battle may shift elsewhere—for example, to bowel movements or to eating, where children do have the last word. Or, worst of all, the battle may go underground and breed a deep pool of anger and resentment to be expressed later, elsewhere, and in nasty ways.

But normally, if parents respect their children's right to rule their own bodies by not bringing in the heavy artillery when children do occasionally defy them, any deep need they feel to constantly reassert their independence gets defused. It becomes a nonissue. When they don't have to constantly defend their autonomy, children are free to be cooperative—most of the time.

But if they flat out defy you, doesn't that make them feel that they have defeated your authority? Doesn't that make them feel that they are now free to do whatever they want?

No. This is a major parental misconception. One instance of absolute disobedience does not undo the fabric of control, because the day-to-day demands and expectations *never* disappear. Tomorrow and the next day and forever, Zachary's father will still ask him to put away his crayons. And because there is no deep autonomy issue that constantly needs to be reasserted, Zachary's overall wish to please wins out. Usually. Zachary would certainly be very pleased if no demands were ever made of him. But that is not going to happen, and he knows it.

By learning that nothing terrible happens when they absolutely defy you, children win their battle—*I am the boss of me*—but you also win yours. The day-to-day demands do not go away.

With most instances of direct defiance, all that is needed is to repeat calmly a request, and *not* get into a battle of wills.

Not useful:

"Zachary, would you please pick up your crayons?"
"I don't want to. I'm too tired."
"Zachary, please pick up your crayons."
"No. I'm not gonna. I'm too tired."
"Zachary, PICK UP YOUR CRAYONS!"
"I won't."
"Zachary! Now. I mean it."
"I won't."
"You're asking for it, Zachary."
"I won't."
"Forget TV tonight."
"I don't care."

Better:

"Zachary, would you please pick up your crayons?"
"I don't want to. I'm too tired."
"Zachary, please pick up your crayons."
"No. I'm not. I'm too tired."

But then Zachary's father says no more. He *waits*. He has made his request and that request still stands. And what usually happens with the Zacharys of the world is that after establishing, at that very moment, *I'm not your slave*, they then do comply. But not right away and not until they have proved *I will do it because I choose to.*

It is important for children to know that their parents are in charge of their lives. But it is equally important for them to know that they are in charge of directing their bodies.

But there are times when you may not have the time or inclination to wait them out. Let's say, for example, that guests are about to arrive and the Tiny Trucks are on the hallway floor.

"Lydia, please pick up your Tiny Trucks. Grandma's coming over soon, and I need the trucks picked up right away."

"But I can't. My arm hurts."

"Lydia, I need the trucks picked up now."

"But my arm hurts."

At this point, what I recommend is that Lydia's mother pick up the Tiny Trucks herself. She does not have the time to wait out her daughter. But what she also needs to do is to make clear to Lydia that she failed to do what was her responsibility.

"Lydia, I don't have time to wait for you to pick up your toys. It was your job and now I have to do it."

But Lydia's mother can't pick up the Tiny Trucks. If she does then she's letting Lydia get away with not picking them up. Lydia's mother can't do that.

As long as Lydia's mother makes it clear to her daughter that she has failed to do her job, and if Lydia's mother continues to make similar demands in the future, Lydia is not getting away with anything. The proof is what real children in real situations do when their parents criticize them for not doing something that they were asked to do.

"Ingrid," says her father, "I asked you to bring in the kindling for the fire and you didn't. I had to. I asked you, but I had to do it."

"I was gonna if you let me. You didn't give me enough time. I was gonna. It's your fault I didn't do it."

Children attempt to fend off the bad feeling that has now invaded their bodies as a result of the criticism. In fact, it is not unusual for children who have failed to do something and were criticized for it actually to pursue a parent, badgering them to try to get them to undo the criticism, to remove the guilt they now feel inside.

What they would like to hear is:

"You're right, Ingrid. I'm sorry. It was thoughtless of me to bring in the kindling and not give you enough of a chance. Please forgive me."

What they get instead is a lingering guilt that eventually goes away, but not without having a definite influence on them in the future—though again probably not enough to guarantee Ingrid will bring in the wood the next time without a fuss. This is why parents do need to persist.

"I do not want to have to bring in the wood like I did last time. It needs to be brought in now."

As always, you want to avoid letting your child suck you into any subsequent baby-self arguments that keep the basic parental message from getting through. The basic message you want to give is:

"You didn't do what I asked. It was your responsibility. And I don't like that."

Talks about responsibility and how as a family you all need to work together are good. Such dialogue can create a family environment of shared and mutual responsibility, which is excellent. But such family togetherness is not the bottom line here. To repeat: if you want your children to regularly do what they do not feel like doing, then you have to make the demand regularly and then persist, both by being there and by remaking the demand on a regular basis. And you must recognize their efforts when they do what is asked.

One fact is inescapable. The earlier you start this regimen in a child's life the more success you will have as they get older. Trying to get teenagers to do regularly what they have never done is obviously going to be a very tough job.

In any event, nothing happens without significant expenditure of parental energy. Children, on their own, do not automatically do what they don't feel like doing. If you want things to get done, you are going to have to invest time and energy. A *lot* of time and energy. Sometimes more time and energy than most parents have. Nor would you want to spend all of your time and energy if it comes at the expense of positive parent-and-child time. In reality, as with so much of child raising, you have to pick and choose what you care about and what you don't care about quite so much. As a result, not all of those tasks you care about are always going to get done.

One last point: the amount of compliance you get can depend on the temperament of a given child. Some are easy, some are not so easy.

"Rashid, please pick up your shirt."
"I can't. Besides, it's not hurting anything."
"Rashid, why can't you be like your sister?"

"Mommy, is there anything more I can do for you? I'll pick up Rashid's shirt and then I can refold the napkins if you want me to. I can make them neater. Would you like me to do that for you, Mommy?"

Children differ. Some require more parental energy than others. But it is a mistake for parents to *really* tighten the screws with the less obedient siblings simply in order to get them in line—in line, for example, with a much more coop-erative sibling. Rather, one has to accept that levels of compli-ance will differ. Ultimately, you must live with what you get.

The Rewards of Persistence

There is consolation. What often can feel like shouting into a blizzard with no effect at all—"Chantal, please don't track mud into the house"—does have an effect.

When growing up, my son, Nick, had the job of bringing in the empty trash barrels on Wednesday afternoons. This job was probably assigned to him when he was seven or eight, nine at the oldest. I would bring the full barrels out in the morning, but it was Nick's job to bring the empty ones into the garage when he got home from school. This was not a very difficult task. The trash barrels were plastic and not heavy, and the distance they had to be carted was maybe twenty feet. But without fail, every Wednesday evening when I returned from work, there would be the trash barrels still at the curb. I would either bring them in or call Nick when I got into the house and tell him to bring them in. He would do it without any significant complaint. Nick had accepted that it was his job. He just didn't do it.

This went on literally for years. Then, one Wednesday evening when Nick was about fifteen, I came home from work to find that the trash barrels were not there. Immediately I assumed, as would most parents in my situation, *Omigod, somebody stole our trash barrels*. But then I happened to look in the garage and there they were.

In the house I immediately called to Nick and asked him, "What's with the trash barrels?"

He said, looking at me as if he didn't know what was I talking about, "Yeah, I brought them in."

"Nick, you brought in the trash barrels?"

And Nick, looking at me like I was a total idiot, even though this was the first time he had ever brought the trash barrels in said, "Yeah, it's my job."

And from then on, although certainly with some lapses, Nick brought in the empty trash barrels every Wednesday afternoon. What I have always made of this, which I think is correct, is that the demand to bring in the trash barrels did go into Nick's developing conscience; he accepted it as his responsibility. But until he was fifteen or so he simply had not had the maturity to follow through. When he was back home from school in the afternoon, luxuriating in full baby-self mode, the effort to switch back to his mature self, however briefly, had just been too great.

A lot of the parenting that we do may at times seem fruitless, but our children do take it in. It does become a part of them. But often it is only when they reach sufficient maturity that we finally get to see the fruits of our labor.

Differences Age by Age

I have said that the baby self does not change over time. Its issues are always the same—it wants only total pleasure, no stress, and, especially when not getting its way, it will not separate. Hence the basic rule for dealing with baby selves when they are not getting their way—whether it be two-year-old baby selves or forty-two-year-old baby selves—is the same. Decide fast, stand firm, and once you have truly taken a stand, do not pick up on anything further that they may throw at you. This rule is absolute and does not change over time. But obviously children do.

As they get older, as a part of normal development, they turn more and more to the world out there and less to parents for their happiness and sense of well being. Baby-self

Baby-Self Album 2

The Baby Self at Home

The Baby Self's Favorite CDs

The Baby Self Cares About How It Looks

**The Baby Self Lets Its Mother Have a Conversation
with Her Friend Eileen**

The Baby Self Takes On Responsibility

The Baby Self Lets Matters Drop

The Baby Self Is *Never* Embarrassed

nurturing—what you can give to them—though always important, is no longer the sole source of their feeling good about themselves. What goes on in the realm of the mature self—learning skills and having friends—takes on ever increasing importance. In what follows I will discuss the main distinctive issues that come up for different age groups and how these play out day to day.

Two to Four

As discussed earlier, with toddlers you cannot rely on your words for obedience. You should make demands—say the words—"Please stop banging your spoon" or "Please stop pinching the baby's foot"—but compliance must rely on you. With toddlers if you want it to happen, you have to get up, go over—and do it fast. They are simply too young for you to count on their having the controls, on their taking the responsibility for their actions all on their own.

Words are of limited usefulness in dealing with their disappointment, also.

"I want to see Gramma and Boppy," sobbed Suki. Suki's mother was running late with too many errands still to finish. The planned visit was no longer possible—which resulted in Suki having a fit.

The secret with disappointed toddlers is that you do not want to try too hard to resolve, to fix, their disappointments—to somehow appease their frustration. It is far better to be loving and sympathetic, but to move on. Hugs and tender words can go a long way toward resolving many disappointments. But regardless, one of the nice things about toddlers is that for them small tragedies do rapidly become history. They move on to whatever is next.

You do want to use words.

"I know you're sad. We don't have time now, but we will go another time."

Although with toddlers such words have little immediate effect as consolation, they do provide a framework for learning to deal with disappointment. *Now is not good but later will be good again.*

What is most important for parents to understand with this stage in life is the primacy of autonomy issues. Probably the biggest and most far-reaching mistake that parents can make with toddlers is entering too frequently into battles of will.

"Tina, come here so I can straighten your hat."

Tina who hates to have her hat straightened stands glaring at her mother and will do so into eternity rather than come over to get her hat straightened.

"Tina, get over here now or else."

Much better is either to forget it, or go over and straighten the hat. But too frequent compliance battles with toddlers can set a bad pattern for the future. The risk is that as they get older all demands, rather than simply being requests to do what they may not feel like doing, again bring up the never ending issue of—*they are trying to boss me around*—an issue they must defend against over and over again, a permanent chip on their shoulder. It makes life so much more difficult.

Hence, not:

"You pick that up, or else."

Or:

"You stop that banging, or else."

But rather:

"Please pick that up," or "Please stop that banging."

And then either wait—and if they don't do it let them know your displeasure, but not too much displeasure:

"Krystal, I don't like it when I ask you to pick up your toys and you don't."

Or, as described, quick physical intervention. Battles of will with toddlers are not where you want to go.

Four to Six

As they move out of the toddler stage they get bigger, quicker, and smarter. Physical intervention, though still possible for many situations (a necessity where there is any risk of harm), is now often less of an option.

"Iris, give me that ball."
"No," says Iris, who quickly ducks into the space behind the sofa, avoiding her mother's grab.

More and more past the age of four you have to switch to Plan B: *make demands, stay put, and wait.* Gradually, it is that plan that comes to replace forever the *act fast* rule of dealing with toddlers.

It is also by this age that the earlier, angry baby-self responses—screaming, crying, tantrums—though occasionally resorted to, start being replaced by more sophisticated verbalizing such as "I hate you," "You're mean," and, everybody's favorite, "Why?" Significant cognitive advances mean that they start to understand not just how *they* feel, but also how other people feel—which is good. But this also means that when they are mad at you, and because they know you love them— which is also good—they want to hurt your feelings. They bring in not only verbal attacks but sulking: *I'm going to make you suffer by being mad at you.*

Once they reach four, most children have begun to put controls on their own behavior—if not always successfully. They know about being good and bad—what Mommy or Daddy says is okay, and what they say is not okay. They begin to develop a conscience. But young consciences see things in a very black-and-white manner. You do bad stuff—bad things happen to you. And young consciences tend to exaggerate— regardless of what parents may say or do—how bad those consequences will be.

That is not all they worry about. By four they begin to notice some very obvious facts. Autonomy—I am my own person separate from Mommy and Daddy—has a price. Their increasing awareness and knowledge of the world they live in reveals a rather serious problem.

I am four and rather tiny and on my own and I really don't stand a chance against rather larger tigers, robbers, and aliens.

The main fear for toddlers is that Mommy or Daddy might leave—I will be alone. But by age four they have a new fear that stays for the rest of their lives. *The world has lots of scary stuff, and if I venture out into it, terrible things might happen to me, which is all the more reason why I don't want to leave Mommy or Daddy.* A whole raft of additional fears starts to become a part of their lives. They can become clingy— which includes starting fights with you for no apparent reason, where they had not before. They may resist going out into all kinds of situations—old and new. What do you do?

First—despite fears, despite clinging—you want to make sure that your child goes out into the world and *continues* to go out, despite what at times can be their considerable resistance.

"Mommy, don't leave me," Roman sobs hysterically as his mother drops him off at nursery school. But that is exactly what she does—drops him off at school and, after a quick hug, exits. And within two minutes he's fine—enjoying nursery school as he always does—which does not stop him from sobbing hysterically the next day.

Second—you can reassure:

"Don't worry, sweetheart, there are no monsters that will come out and kill you after you go to bed in your room."

"You'll see, you'll have a good time at the birthday party."

But your greatest reassurance to your children is not in the words that you might say, but in your confidence that nothing terrible will happen and your willingness—despite the fact that you totally love them—to expose them to those situations that they may so fear and resist. *You* are not worried.

Six to Nine

By the time they enter grade school, their life at home and your love and support remain crucial for their happiness and well being. But by now you alone can no longer make them fully happy. Parental love cannot meet all of their emotional needs. Their competence away from home and their ability to have friends now has major importance as well.

As their accomplishments, or lack thereof, take on increasing significance for them, that world—school and being with friends—becomes both a source of gratification and of stress. Home increasingly becomes a place to unwind. One result is that home and school behavior—the mature and baby selves—can become *very* noticeably different.

By grade school often you can begin to see a frequent pattern with many well-functioning kids. They put demands on themselves—they do strive to do well in school, they do put curbs on their behavior while out in the world, they do genuinely try to do the best that they can, all of which takes considerable effort. Of their own choosing they put significant stress on themselves as they go out into the world. But then they come home. I often picture it like a guitar or violin string wound tight during the day. Once they are in the door, they completely let go. And you get the backlash.

"Mitchell, please try not to track mud in the house."
"Why do you always have to yell at me about stuff. You always do. You yell at me all the time. You do."

"Sacha, how was school today, sweetheart?"
"It was terrible. It's always terrible. I don't know why kids have to go to school. I have a headache. Why isn't there anything to eat here?"

What is their problem? Just that they are doing a little unwinding after a hard day at the office.

There is a paradox. Many seem to *want* to engage in arguments. And your stress level rises. But were we to hook them up to some sort of stress-o-meter, actually measure their stress level while they are fussing at you, we would see theirs going down, well below the level that they had endured while at school. We want them to have a place to unwind, to soak up nurturing. It is good for them. They need it. But sometimes that unwinding can be at your expense.

Occasionally it can get a little confusing.

"Carole Ann, please pick up your toys now. It's almost supper."

"I'll do it after."

"No, Carole Ann, I want it done now."

"I'll do it after. I said I'll do it after. You don't know. I always have too much stuff to do. It's too hard. I do stuff here. I have to do stuff at school. School's too hard. It is."

Does Carole Ann have a problem in school? Is school too hard? Should her father be concerned? Maybe there's a problem. Maybe there's not. Regardless, the rule, as always, is—do not go into it then. The problem *then* is toys that need to be picked up before supper.

"Carole Ann, please pick up your toys now."

As always, if you are concerned, talk about it later.

"Carole Ann, are you having trouble in school?"

"No, not really, Daddy. It's just sometimes it's hard."

Or maybe:

"I don't know. When Mrs. Eaglegarden gives us instructions, I get confused a lot."

Sometimes there is a real problem. Sometimes you will get to know about it and you may be able to help. But often they can be extra crabby, go through rough periods, and you never do know whether something is truly bothering them or whether they are just going through the normal occasional crabby period. You cannot always know.

A fact about your children once they reach grade school is that there is now much in their life over which you have little or no control. Sadnesses will come into their lives. Bad things will happen to them. They will not always be able to succeed as you want them to. Sometimes—because of what goes on out there in the world—they do genuinely suffer. And you cannot always make it better. But nonetheless, whatever is going on out there, one option that you do not have is to allow them to withdraw.

"Sweetheart."
"Yes, Dad."
"Your mother and I have decided that life out there is just too hard. So we've decided that you can stay home forever."
"Cool."

Regardless of failures, regardless of problems, regardless of situations that despite your efforts you cannot fix, you have to keep putting them out there anyway. There is no choice. Luckily, in real life, problems do have a way of being resolved, or if not, of becoming part of the past. And a lot that they resist may not be as bad as it seems. That also means that it is a good idea to be tough about not letting them quit activities they seem to complain about if you feel that they are actually capable of handling them.

"But I hate soccer."

Far more often than not where kids ended up quitting, parents when looking back, wish they hadn't let them.

And no, you should not ease up on making them pick up their toys before supper.

Nine to Twelve

This is an age group that sometimes seems a little hard to define. Certainly one effect of the huge role that media has in children's lives, their greater access to the culture at large, is that preteens today seem to take on many seemingly adolescent characteristics. But very definitely they are not adolescents. By nine or ten one major change that has occurred is that they are truly far more competent. They have mastered many skills. There is much that they can do on their own, sometimes better than their parents. It is at this stage of their lives that they are probably at their most confident. They do have confidence in their own abilities, but simultaneously they still rest secure within the all-embracing arms of Mommy and Daddy. *They will take care of me. I don't have to worry about that.* The tie is still very much there. If there are big problems, they do not feel that they have to deal with them on their own. They can still turn to Mommy or Daddy. They are not independent and that is just fine with them.

What is perhaps the toughest problem for parents in dealing with kids in this age group is that they become more bold. It's not that they disobey more—they usually don't—but their words, their arguing, their tone of voice can be far more challenging than before.

"What gives you the right?"

Swearing, though not often directed at you, may be heard much more at home. Before, when their baby selves were not getting their way their utterances were often provocative, hard to ignore. But in these years before adolescence what they say can scream out that they must be responded to—immediately. But all that leads to is trouble.

"I didn't ask for you to be my parents."

"How can you say that after all that your father and I have done for you?"

"What? What have you done except always tell me to do stuff and yell at me and compare me to Miss Perfect Allison?"

But for all their seeming surface adolescentlike behavior, they are *not* teenagers. They are not yet truly moving away from you. It can just sound that way. What this means is that if you stick to your guns, do not get sidetracked by their now *really* provocative baby self, what you do will work. You do not have major rebellions on your hands. They are still kids, kids who very much want and accept their parents, who are there to love and protect them. They have no interest at all in jeopardizing that.

Yet by this stage their lives can get to be overwhelming at times. There is a lot being asked of them. More and harder work in school. Having friends now takes on more importance; the concept of popularity increases the pressure to fit in. It is hard. They still very much need and crave their baby-self place. And they still do need you. Giving preteens hugs on a regular basis is a good idea, is accepted, appreciated, and fills a real need—even if they don't always show it. Though they may at times look like they no longer need you, they very much still do.

Adolescence

Though this book is not written for parents of adolescents, most everything in it does apply with teenagers. It is just that it does not work as well. I have often—only half jokingly—compared parenting younger kids to having a steering wheel. Sometimes the steering wheel is easy to turn, sometimes hard, occasionally you may even lose control. With teenagers you also have a steering wheel, it is just that it is not connected to anything. This doesn't mean that they don't do what you want—sometimes they do. It is just that it doesn't seem to be because of anything that you are doing.

Also the stakes go up—drugs, sex, drinking, trying to prepare them for the now all-too-soon time that they will—hopefully—be out on their own. And not only do the stakes go up, but the defining psychological force of adolescence kicks in. As part of normal development, it is no longer acceptable for them to experience themselves as dependent little children. They now must see themselves as independent adultlike beings. Parents, just by their presence, let alone by their demands, now make them feel belittled. They push away—constantly.

How do you prepare yourself and your children against the inevitable coming of adolescence? By doing exactly what you are doing. All of the good things that you do as a parent make a huge positive difference once they reach adolescence.

You cannot ensure that no problems will come. Some certainly will. But just by being a loving, strong parent you make the odds very much in your favor that the greater disasters will not strike. They will reach adulthood still in one piece.

III

Day to Day

Unpleasantness from Their Mouths

Much of what kids say can be a source of delight—loving, funny, extraordinarily innocent, even profound—but as any parent knows, much of what comes out of their mouths can be extraordinarily unpleasant and aggravating as well. In regard to these unpleasant utterances of the baby self, you can make a huge difference. You can dramatically reduce—though never eliminate—most verbal baby-self unpleasantness.

Whining

I start with whining because perhaps nowhere in the realm of child raising is the effectiveness of *nonresponse* so clearly and absolutely demonstrated. With whining, you have three options:

1) Respond as if they were speaking normally.

"Mom, I can't button my sleeve," whines Esteban.
"Come here, Esteban. I'll see if I can help."

2) In some manner instruct your child not to whine.

"Stop whining! You know how I hate it when you whine."

Or:

"I am not going to listen to you when you whine."

Or:

"Say it without whining, and maybe I'll help you with your button."

3) Absolutely ignore the whining as if the child were not speaking at all.

"Mom, I can't button my sleeve," whines Esteban.
Silence
"Mom, I can't button my sleeve," whines Esteban even more insistently.
Silence

With the first two responses, the whining will continue as part of a child's behavior. With the third response, if adhered to absolutely, always and without exception, children will not be whiners. Nonresponse is so effective because whining comes directly from the heart of the baby self. Since what the baby self eats for food is parental response, if whining produces nothing, receives nothing in return from parents, it will wither and die. Any parent who has tried very hard but unsuccessfully to stop their children's whining will truly appreciate the power of nonresponse.

Complaining

Complaining is more or less the same as whining, but it differs slightly in that it's one step up, developmentally. Complaints come from older kids whose fussing relies on the meaning of their words rather than on the maddening tone of their voice.

Some complaints are legitimate and require our attention.

"Mommy, my glasses keep pinching my ear!"

And indeed there are red marks behind Samantha's ears, and her glasses require an adjustment in the fit. But many complaints—and the difference is easy to tell—are simply about the current state of affairs in their lives, designed to pull you into a warm, tasty, and endless baby-self fuss.

As you will see in the following dialogues, there really are two opposite ways of dealing with complaining. The first, which will receive much baby-self applause, will also get you sucked right into the complaint. The second, in effect, gently tosses the complaint right back to the child—friendly, even sympathetic, but, from the standpoint of the baby self, useless.

Golly, that's a problem for you, isn't it? But it's not a problem for me, and not a problem I have even the slightest intention of doing anything about.

Eight-year-old Deedee, beginning to eat her supper:

"This stew is too salty. I can't eat it." The stew is no more salty than it usually is, and Deedee usually eats it, although it definitely is not one of her favorite suppers.

"Well, dear, it's what's for supper."

"But I can't eat it."

"Well, that's what's for supper."

"But I can't eat this. It's too salty. I want something else."

"I'm not going to make you something else. This is what's for supper, and you're just going to have to learn to eat some things you don't like."

"Well, I'm not going to eat this. It's too salty. It makes me want to throw up. I want something else."

"I'm not going to make you something else."

"But I'll be hungry. I hate this stew. It's gross."

Deedee's mother should not get caught up in her daughter's complaining. If she wishes, she can make her daughter something else. But if she chooses not to:

"This stew is too salty. I can't eat it."

"I'm sorry you don't like the stew, dear."

Note that the words don't challenge Deedee, but simply echo her complaint: "Yes, you don't like the stew."

"But I can't eat it. Make me something else."

"Gosh, I guess you won't eat the stew, then."

"But it's too salty. You have to make me something else."

But again, Deedee's mother disengages very early. She has given her daughter the choice of eating the stew or not. It's up to her. But Deedee's mother is neither going to make her anything new nor deal with the complaint any further.

"Yuck. I'm almost choking on it. Ugh, it's so salty."

But if this gets no response, it is surprising how swiftly it dies and how swiftly they move on.

"Cloverly told me today in school that her dog is so sick that they might have to put it to sleep."

"That will be sad for Cloverly."

"Yeah, he's a nice dog."

And maybe Deedee eats the stew and maybe she doesn't, but the complaining ends.

Another example:

"Mom, J.J. keeps drooling."

"Stop drooling, J.J."

"I'm not drooling. Carla's lying."

"He is drooling, Mom. Look."

"J.J., stop teasing your sister."

"I'm not doing anything. Carla's such a liar."

"I'm not a liar. You're a liar. Mom, tell him to stop. He's disgusting."

"J.J., it is disgusting. Please stop it."

"I'm not doing anything to her. She doesn't have to look."

"See, Mom, the little liar admits he was drooling."

"If I can't drool, tell Carla not to do the thing with her eyes at me."

"Carla, don't do the thing with your eyes at your brother."

"Tell him not to pick his nose."

I will have more to say shortly about sibling fighting. But this charming dialogue illustrates one obvious point. Try to resolve sibling squabbles and all you will get is a feeding frenzy by *two* baby selves, both enthusiastically coming back for more.

"Mom, J.J. keeps drooling."
"Gosh, that sounds unpleasant."
"Well, tell him to stop."

But at that point, unless the children's mother wants to intervene, which is basically only asking for trouble, there really is nothing more to say. There is no answer to Carla's demand. Instead, their mother should just go about her business.

"But you have to make him stop . . . Mom, make him stop . . . Mom, you're not listening."

Which is exactly right. She isn't listening anymore. At least not to anything that has to do with the Carla-and-J.J.-drooling story.

Interrupting

Nicole's mother is sitting in her kitchen having a cup of coffee with her friend Vivian.

"So I said to Clarence, 'This is so ridiculous.' And what does he do but—"
"Mom, will you play cards with me?"
"Nicole, I'm talking to Vivian."
"But I don't have anything to do."
"Nicole, how many times do I have to tell you not to interrupt when I'm talking to somebody else?"
"But Mom, there really is nothing to do. I'm going to get crabby."
"Nicole, I am talking to Vivian."
"But Mom, I don't know what to do. You have to do something with me. You have to."

Interrupting is not good. It comes from a particularly un-pleasant piggy and controlling side of the baby self. What to do about it is fairly straightforward. You need to be tough. If it is a legitimate request, attend to it.

"Mom, I can't get the top off the peanut butter jar."

Otherwise:

1. Do not drop what you are doing to engage your child. If you do so, she will have gotten what she wanted and the interrupting will continue.
2. Interrupt your conversation only to say, "I am talking to Vivian. You can talk to me later," or "I am on the phone." But say no more.
3. If the child persists, which she usually will, repeat step 2: "I am talking to Vivian."
4. If she still persists, which she often will, sometimes to the point where she interferes with your ability to carry on the conversation, say "Excuse me," take your child to another part of the room, and say, "You may not interrupt me," and then immediately resume your conversation. This usually works, but if they further persist they will need to be tem-porarily banned from being in the room with you.

Later, if you wish, speak to them about the interrupting.

"I do not want you interrupting when I am talking to someone else."

Overall, this procedure will work. If all that your kids ever get from their interrupting is a stern, repetitious version of you and nothing more, learning that they cannot pull you away from a conversation, they will for the most part quit trying.

Back Talk

Perhaps the biggest problem with back talk is that it seems to break a moral law:

Children should respect their parents.

Parents feel obligated to pick up on it:

As a citizen of the United States of America, it is my duty to my country not to let my child get away with talking back.

Yet there is a basic truth about back talk, assuming that the children do not fear harsh reprisal: if a parent's true aim is to reduce back talk to a minimum, the most effective response is not to respond at all, and then to move on.

"No, Aaron, the TV goes off now and no more fussing."
"You're the one that's fussing."
"Aaron, please turn off the TV."

But saying nothing to back talk, isn't that saying that the back talk is okay?

No, it does not. What it says to a child is:

Your back talk is completely ineffective at getting anything further from me.

When you pick up on back talk, no matter what your words, no matter what it is that you might intend to teach, what you say is always:

Your back talk does get a response from me. It is effective in producing more involvement.

Because you are dealing with the baby self, that is what responding to back talk teaches. Nothing else.

But then you are allowing back talk.

In not responding to back talk, by not bringing in the threat of harsh punishment, the threat of harsh reprisal, you are indeed allowing it. But allowing and approving are not the same thing. If you disapprove of their back talk, let them know. As with other infractions, do it later. But, still, unless you are willing to bring in real fear, some back talk will continue. They know it is wrong but they do not feel that it is very wrong.

Does back talk from children mean that children do not respect their parents?

That's a foolish question. Of course it does.

Maybe not. If respect means *fear*, then children today, who do not have the same kind of fear of their parents felt by earlier generations, do not respect their parents. But if respect means admire and "look up to," then that is a whole other story. Parents would be surprised. Children today do say— especially to others outside the family (and so long as there is no current issue where they are not getting their way)—that they love their parents, think they are good parents, know and appreciate that they are there for them, admire and look up to them. Kids today do respect their parents. It's just that they do not fear them.

With the approach to back talk that I am recommending

here, I am making a value judgment about respectful behavior. I am saying that children's back talk to their parents is of a distinctly lesser order of bad. Where I choose to draw my line is at respectful, polite behavior toward others, especially adults, in the world out there. In keeping with the reality of the two worlds of the baby and the mature self, I differentiate between home and family, and out there.

This was the line that Mary Alice and I chose to draw with our kids. I can only say that from an early age Nick and Margaret, without much effort on our part, had two very clear standards of behavior. They were kids who we could and did confidently take out in public and to other people's houses. They could and would differentiate between close friends and guests with whom we were on more formal terms. The close friends might get a dose of baby-self acting out now and then.

No matter where you choose to draw your line, there remains one inescapable fact about back talk to parents. The less you respond at the time, the less you get. The more you respond, the more you get.

Swearing

"#!%$!"

This is another real winner. All a child has to do is to say any of a number of magic words and an argument that has ended gets to start up again. Defeat turns into triumph.

"That's it, Patrick. I have nothing more to say."
"#!%$!"
"Don't you dare talk to me that way."
"I will too. You're not fair."
"You will not use those words with me."
"Yes, I will. You can't stop my mouth."

"We'll see about what I can stop."
Etc.

To children, swear words are remarkable. Just by saying them they can immediately invoke a major response from their parent. As discussed earlier, I am not saying a parent should not respond at the time. They may feel that a particular remark just goes too far. But I am saying that in doing so, they do reenter the argument, do start the battle anew, and do risk undoing what they may have just accomplished.

If you want to effect whether and how much swearing you will get, as always it is far better to bring it up later.

"I do not like your using that kind of language with me."

The truth is kids today do not view swear words as being as naughty as did kids of a couple of generations ago. It is an overall societal change. This said, my experience has been that in those homes where parents truly believe that the swearing is wrong, the children usually do swear far less—at least at home.

9

Baby-Self Favorites

As discussed, the baby self is very smart and possesses exactly the same brain as the mature self. Baby selves worldwide are very tuned in to their parents and have hit upon many especially effective ways to achieve their goals, usually either getting you to change your mind or, just as happily, engaging you in an endless fuss. Here are the baby self's all-time favorites.

It's Not Fair

This is perhaps the baby self's favorite complaint of all.

"It's not fair. Yesterday, James got to play Death Wand 600 for over an hour. Why do I have to stop now?"

"Simon, it's getting close to your bedtime and I need you to stop so you can start getting ready for bed."

"But it's not fair. James got to play for over an hour yesterday. It's not fair."

The problem, of course, is that we do want to be fair. We want to be fair to our children because we want to teach them to be fair themselves.

"That's right. I agree with the author. You have to let me play as long as James did or else it's not fair. If you don't let me, I'll grow up all warped and unfair, and I'll probably cheat on my income tax."

But we don't *always* have to be fair. Overall, yes, but there are times when what is fair can be too hard to figure out, and other times—more of these—when you just don't have the time to worry about fairness. Parenting efficiency, at times, needs to supercede fairness. Best is not to worry about it.

"Simon, you have to stop now and get ready for bed."
"But it's not fair."
"You heard what I said."

For a parent to be held to perfect fairness simply does not work.

"I know what we'll do, Simon. We'll buy a time clock that adds up all the minutes that you and James play Death Wand 600 and that way we can make sure that you and he will get the exact same amount of time."
"But that still won't be fair, because he always gets the better times."

Perfect fairness just does not work.

Well, then, how do they learn fairness?

If we try to be completely fair all of the time, what our children will learn is how to be very good lawyers, and also how to run us into the ground whenever we try to take a stand. It does not work. They learn fairness because *in general* we are fair, and we do try to be fair with them, and this comes through to them. But moment by moment we cannot always be completely fair.

"But you have to be fair. It's the law. I have to get the same amount of time as James. You have to be fair. Don't listen to the author. He's wrong."

But You Let Phillip

This is an obvious, tried-and-true variation on "It's not fair." The baby self, with its extraordinary memory for all things that ever happened that might be to its slightest advantage, swiftly jumps on this one. It must yield the same response as "It's not fair."

"But you let Phillip do it when he was ten," an irate Melinda screams at her mother.

Maybe her mother let Phillip do it when he was ten, maybe she didn't. But either way she definitely does not want to touch the comparison issue. To allow a comparison with a sibling as a possible bargaining chip opens the floodgates for endless bickering. Instead, stay with this particular child, in this particular here and now.

"No, Melinda, you may not do it."
"But you let Phillip when he was ten."
"No, Melinda, you may not do it."

Surprisingly, despite the overwhelming sense of injustice they feel at the time, if bringing in the comparison to another sibling consistently bears no fruit, they do not persist. The baby self cares nothing about fairness. All it cares about is winning. If making comparisons to siblings doesn't work, it will try something else.

I Hate You

Another real winner for the baby self is "I hate you," which is often used interchangeably with "You're mean."

"Stop popping Bradley with the dish towel."
"But he started it."
"Stop it right now!"
"You never tell Bradley to stop anything. You don't. I hate you."

We briefly considered "I hate you" when discussing the characteristics of the baby self. But since it is such a favorite, it's worth revisiting.

Words like this can really hurt, but they shouldn't. Of course the baby self hates you and thinks you're mean. You're the one who is causing it not to get its way. The baby self only deals in now, and right now it doesn't like you. Not at all. The baby self says what it feels, and what it feels is that it wants to get back at you for making it feel bad—which you did, by not letting it get its way.

But does your child really hate you? Does he really think you are the meanest person on earth? Of course not. He loves you as always. Also, he feels he can say mean things to you because he feels totally safe in your love, that what he says risks nothing in whether you will continue to love him or not. What they say may *seem* terrible, but, in fact, what it really means is that they are totally comfortable with you and certain of your love. And this is exactly what you want them to feel.

If you don't want them—their baby selves—ever to hate you, what's your alternative?

"I'm sorry, dear. I shouldn't have stopped you from popping your brother with the dishtowel. He did deserve it. Here's the towel back, dear."

"Cool! Bradley, I have a surprise for you."

You Don't Love Me

Here the baby self really doesn't play fair.

Winston's father had just angrily reprimanded his son for intentionally stepping on his sister's crayons.

"You don't love me," sobbed Winston, literally slobbering as the tears poured down.

"How can you say that?" said his father. "You know I do."

"No, you don't. You don't love me," again sobbed Winston, choking on his tears as he cried.

The irony of "You don't love me" is that children who seriously might think at some level that a parent might not love them would *never* say it. The actual thought in a child's mind that their parent might not love them is much too devastating, too terrifying, ever to bring up directly. Basically, children who say it do so *precisely* because they know that their parents do love them. Hence, "You don't love me" really means:

I know you love me, which is why I'm saying the opposite because I know it will upset you, which is what I want to do because I'm mad at you.

But, as always, you can't touch this diversionary tactic. Stay on the subject.

"I don't like that you stepped on Safiya's crayons on purpose."
"See! See! You don't love me."

But his father does see and says no more.

I Can't Do Anything Right

This one is perhaps the most subtle tactic in the baby self's basic repertoire. If too effective, this one can create problems for the child as well as for the parent.

"Oscar, come here and take out the trash now. Why do I have to get after you all the time to do your job? When are you going to learn a little responsibility?"
"You're always yelling at me. I can't ever please you. I can't ever do anything right. I'm just a big failure, aren't I?"

The problem with this tactic is that it hits at a real fear of parents:

Is my child unhappy?

"How can you say that, Oscar? You're not a failure. It's just that we sometimes get mad that we have to keep after you to do things."
"No, you and Mom are disappointed in me. You wish I was different."
"That's not true, Oscar."
"Yes, it is. I'm a loser."

Now, of course, the whole topic has changed from the unpleasant subject of trash that needs to be taken out to one that is far more pleasing to the baby self. But the unhappiness ploy works only if it is believed by both player and audience.

Many children can lock into a sadness that has no origin other than the effect it produces on their parents. Unfortunately, some children will seek a tie with their parents through sadness. Some, to their own detriment, take advantage of the fact that being sad or upset can get parental attention of a special and pleasing sort. Over time, repeatedly using this ploy, they come to believe it. Their depression is no longer pretend, but becomes real.

But if they truly aren't happy, I certainly don't want to ignore it.

The answer is, as always, to look at *when* you are hearing this complaint of sadness. If it always seems related to times of chores that one tragically has to do, or to episodes of justified parental criticism that are unhappily received, think twice before you pick up on it. If you seriously worry about the issue, ask—but later.

"Oscar, do you really feel that you are a failure, that your mom and I are disappointed in you?"

But when trash needs to be taken out, the wise parent does not touch the sadness.

Why?

"But why? Why? Why can't I? Why? Why not? Why?"

The endless whys can really get under your skin. Assuming that you have already given your best answer to the first why or two, the best course is to ignore any further ones. But anyone who has been on the other side of a "why" attack knows that ignoring it can be tough. So your next best option when they start in is to swiftly separate.

"But why? Why not? Why?"
"Good-bye, Claudia."
"But why? Why?"
"Good-bye, Claudia."
"You never give me reasons."

I Won't/You Can't Make Me

These two are essentially the same and especially beloved by the baby self because they can produce that wonderful baby-self gourmet dish—a battle of wills. I have discussed the issues underlying direct defiance. But in general the most important thing for parents to know about these words of defiance is that with children, the words are not necessarily tied to the intention. *Saying* them costs little. In fact, "I won't" can be a great opener if it successfully obscures the issue of obedience by provoking a delicious fight instead.

"Ruthie, please put away the bubble blower. That's enough bubbles for today."
"I won't."
"What?"
"I won't."
"That's what I thought you said."
"Well, I won't."
"We'll see about that. Give me the bubble blowing stuff now."
"I won't."
"GIVE IT TO ME NOW!"
"I WON'T!"

Ruthie's mother then makes a grab at the bubble blower, misses as Ruthie dodges and then runs out of the room, clutching the bubble blower with her mother in hot pursuit.

The secret is not to bite.

"Ruthie, please put away the bubble blower. That's enough bubbles for today."

"I won't."

"I'm sorry, Ruthie. That's it for bubble blowing."

"I won't. You can't make me."

And Ruthie's mother, having said what she needs to, stands and patiently waits.

"You hate if I have fun," grumbles Ruthie as she puts away the bubble blower and the liquid.

"Thank you," says her mother.

I'm Bored

"I'm bored."

"You can't find anything to do?"

"No, I'm bored. There's nothing to do."

"How about coloring in your new coloring book? You haven't done that in a while."

"Coloring is boring."

"You usually like coloring."

"No, I don't. It's boring. There's nothing to do. You do something with me."

"I'm busy now, Pedro. You're just going to have to find something for yourself to do."

"I can't. I'm too bored. You have to do something with me."

"Well, what about your Build-O-Straws? You haven't

made anything with them for a while. Remember last time you made that cool fortress? I'll bet you could think of something else like that to build."

"No, I can't. The Build-O-Straws are boring. I'm so bored. There's nothing for me to do. You *have* to do something with me."

Virtually all children can entertain themselves. It is just that often they choose not to, because they want you. Being bored is a lot like survival training on a deserted island. Somehow you have to make it through on your own. Unless children have practice in getting through time, they can become wholly dependent on others to get them through it. Rather than trying to be too helpful in solving their what-to-do problems, usually it is best to gently throw it right back to them.

"I'm bored."

"Gosh, Pedro, I guess you'll have to find something to do."

"But there is nothing to do. I'm so bored. You do something with me."

"No, I'm sorry. I'm busy."

"But I'm so bored. There *is* nothing to do."

"Gosh, that's a problem."

"But you have to do something with me, I'm so bored."

"Gosh, I don't know what to tell you."

"You have to tell me what to do. You *have* to do something with me."

But if Pedro's mother holds firm, Pedro will then be on his own.

"I'm bored. I'm bored. I'm bored. I'm so bored. I'm dying of boredom. I think my heart has stopped. I'm bored. I'm bored. I'm bored."

But ultimately being bored does get boring.

"I'm bored. I'm bored. I'm boring. I'm bored." *That's sort of a song.* "I'm boring. I'm boring. I'm bored. I'm bored." *Maybe I can do a tune to it.*

And Pedro on his own goes to the small electronic keyboard that he got for Christmas and works out a melody to his song. He figures out three verses. Writes them down. Figures out a title: "I'm So Bored I Could Die," and then well over an hour having gone by, returns to his mother.

"You have to hear my song," which Pedro then plays for his mother.

It really does work that way. If left on their own children do not sit endlessly rocking back and forth staring at the wall. "I'm bored. I'm bored. I'm bored." Children do have the capacity to entertain themselves. It is just that they often would rather not.

You Promised

Another revered favorite.

"No, I'm sorry, honey. We're just not going to have time to go to the park."

"But you promised!"

"Livia, I didn't promise. I said I thought we could go to the park. It turns out I was wrong. There's not enough time. I'm sorry."

"But you promised."

"I didn't promise, Livia."

"Yes, you did. You promised."

I'm not actually sure what I said to Livia, but I don't think I used the word "promised." But it sort of was like a promise. Actually I don't remember. Maybe I did say "promise."

"You did. You promised. You have to take me to the park."

It is good to keep promises, which is why it's good not to promise something unless you're pretty sure it's going to happen. But the way life works, sometimes things that you plan to do just don't work out. Most parents don't want to break promises, which is why they usually shy away from using that exact word.

"Promise me."
"I can't promise, but I'm pretty sure we will."

But the baby self with its crafty little brain learns at an early age that the word "promise" carries a lot of leverage. And of course the baby self could care less whether a promise was actually made. All it cares about is getting its way.

"But you promised!"

And maybe Livia's mother did and maybe she didn't. But either way:

"I'm sorry, Livia, we're not going."
"BUT YOU PROMISED!"

And no, Livia should not get something extra instead, even if her mother had promised to take her to the park. Life doesn't always work out.

"But she did promise. She really did. I have it on tape. Let me play it for you."

But at Dad's House I Never Have To

With divorced parents this is particularly effective because it can touch a very sensitive place.

That bastard. He's spoiling the kids rotten. Why do I always have to be the bad guy? He undermines everything I do with the kids, just like he did when we were married.

The normal reaction to this provocation is to want to go immediately to the source of the problem.

"Edgar, I know you don't ever want to say 'no' to the kids, but eleven is way too late for them to be staying up, even on weekends. And now they're giving me all kinds of trouble about going to bed over here."

Unfortunately, a typical response to this might be:

"Therese, you know what the best thing is about our divorce? I don't have to listen to you when you try to tell me what to do."

Going to the source usually doesn't work, and it often creates unneeded friction. Unneeded because there is a surprisingly simple solution.

"But at Dad's I get to stay up until eleven."
"How nice for you at your dad's, but here you have to go to bed at nine on Saturday nights."
"But at Dad's . . ."

If "But at Dad's . . ." regularly proves fruitless, if it changes nothing at Mom's, if it fails to get any special response from

Mom, it is surprising how this particular baby-self ploy drops out of the repertoire. But, of course, the baby self never gives up.

"Go to bed at nine? Oh, Mommy, that makes me feel so sad. I feel so sad. Look, feel my tears."

You Never Listen to Me

This is a particularly important weapon in the baby-self arsenal because it directly attacks what the parent is actually doing—not listening.

"No, Tanya, you may not use the blow-dryer on Mr. Muffles." (That's the cat.)
"But it doesn't hurt him. I want to make him all pretty. It doesn't hurt him."
"No, Tanya, you may not blow-dry Mr. Muffles."
"But it won't hurt him. It won't. He likes it."
"You heard me, Tanya."
"But he likes it. He does. It doesn't hurt him. It doesn't . . . You're not listening. You *never* listen to me. You *never* do."

Tanya's baby self is right. Her parent is not listening. Of course the baby self usually adds its extra twist—*never*—which is nothing but baby-self hyperbole.

We do want to listen to our children. Listening is very important. But once a parent has definitely taken a stand, no, we do not want to listen. Listening is for other times. But not now.

"But, Mom, look at this book."
"What is that, Tanya?"
"It's Reginald Peabody's psychiatric classic, *Unlistened-to*

Children: The Roots of Adult Depression. I can feel the seeds being planted in me right now. You have to listen to me."

No, you don't.

Useful Phrases

The baby self's aim—when not getting its way—is to grab hold and not let go. As just described, baby selves use certain well-established parental traps to accomplish the above aim. What you want to do is not snap at their bait. What follows are some useful parent phrases that, rather than take the bait, decline the offering and gently nudge it back into the baby self's lap.

1. Gosh, that's a problem.

"Cameron just hit me, and now he won't give me back my red squishy ball."
"Gosh, that sounds like a problem." (For you, not for me.)
"But he took my red squishy ball."

Which might lead you to:

2. Sounds like you're mad.

"Sounds like you're mad."
"But he took my red squishy ball and he hit me on my bad arm. You have to do something."

Which might lead you to:

3. Gosh, I don't know what to say to you.

"Gosh, I don't know what to say to you."

"But you have to do something! You have to! You have to do something!"

Which might lead you to:

4. Good-bye.

"Good-bye, Joseph."

"But it's not fair. You have to do something. You're not listening to me."

Good Listening

Much in this book is about not listening—specifically when children are not getting their way and their baby self starts in on its endless fussing. But listening to one's children is an important part of child raising. Most of the time we do want to listen. What is so especially good about listening is that it gives children a chance to fill the room with themselves, what they think, care about, their opinions, their stories. Being heard makes them feel important. It is an extremely self-affirming process.

There is a skill to being a good listener. A characteristic of all parents, deeply ingrained within their genetic programming—myself included—is that when their children tell them anything about what is going on in their lives, parents feel the absolute need to turn it into a teaching moment. Sometimes our innate parenting instincts get in the way of our children's chance to be onstage. Sometimes we want to be helpful when what they want is just to tell us.

Geraldine to her mother:

"Mom, I don't like Kristin Wuhlmeyer."

"Why, dear?"

"She's a jerk. She wouldn't give me a turn. She kept hogging the Whirlycycle."

"Did you ask her nicely?"

"Yeah. She just wouldn't. She's a hog."

"Well, maybe you just have to wait longer."

"She will never give it to me. She's a jerk."

"Well, it is her Whirlycycle. Maybe you have to wait until she stops for a while, and then tell her how you would really like to have a turn."

"She's a big pig. She will never give me a turn."

"Well, maybe she won't. Sometimes people just don't want to share no matter how much you ask."

"She's a pig."

"Sometimes you have to go off and find something to do on your own."

"Not with piggy Kristin Wuhlmeyer."

What Geraldine's mother has said was all good and helpful. Her words were an appropriate model for her child's handling of a frustrating situation. But Geraldine only wanted to tell her mother what a big pig Kristin Wuhlmeyer was. At the end of their conversation, Geraldine was dissatisfied with the outcome.

Mom doesn't understand what a big pig Kristin Wuhlmeyer is.

Sometimes the best listening is in staying with what they are saying and *not* going in some other direction even if we feel it might be helpful. Carl Rogers, an influential psychotherapist of the 1950s and 1960s, was a master of good listening. When he responded to his clients, he would repeat to them a shortened, sometimes slightly altered, but often exact version of what they had just said. A typical dialogue would be:

"I went to the store and I had a terrible time. I couldn't find anything I wanted."

"You had a terrible time at the store. You couldn't find anything you wanted."

"That's right. It doesn't seem like it's worth going out sometimes. You never accomplish anything."

"You feel that sometimes going out is a waste of time, as you don't accomplish anything."

"You said it. It gets so depressing some of the time."

"You feel it gets very depressing sometimes."

"Yeah, it does. Like last Thursday with Harold . . ."

I once saw a film of Carl Rogers with a client and he really did say back to her exactly what she had just said. It may seem stupid but the truth is, as any psychotherapist knows, that it's remarkably effective simply to allow people to say what they have to say. The result is very beneficial: they feel they have been heard.

With Geraldine and her mother better listening might have been:

"I don't like Kristin Wuhlmeyer."

"You don't?"

"No, she's a jerk."

"Why? What did she do?"

"She wouldn't give me a turn. She kept hogging the Whirlycycle."

"That was pretty selfish."

"Yeah, she's a big pig. I would like to sock her in the nose."

"You were mad."

"I would like to sock her in the nose twice. She is the biggest pig in the world."

"You were really mad."

"Yeah. What are we having for supper?"

Geraldine was mad because Kristin Wuhlmeyer had hogged the Whirlycycle. She wanted to tell her mother about it and about how mad she was at Kristin Wuhlmeyer. By telling her mother *her* story about Kristin, Geraldine was able to present a part of herself, something that happened to her and what she thought about it. Having told this to her mother, Geraldine had accomplished what she wanted, felt listened to, and had nothing more to say. Her mother had heard her story, understood it, and appreciated it. Geraldine was happy.

Sometimes we definitely do not want to listen to our children. But often we do, and when we do it is often best *just* to listen.

10

Sibling Fighting

Nine-year-old Donald and seven-year-old Daniel were watching TV in the family room when a fight broke out over who was hogging the couch. Shortly, Daniel ran out of the room, crying, with his older brother in pursuit. Daniel went directly to his father.

"Donald won't let me sit on the couch and he keeps hitting me and he twisted my arm real hard and I think he broke it."

"Danny's such a liar. He kept kicking me. I wasn't doing anything."

"I did not. Donald's the one that's lying."

"I'm going to slam you, Danny."

"See, Dad, see?"

At this point their father intervened:

"Calm down, boys. Donald. Danny. Now I want each of you to tell me what went on. One at a time, and no interrupting. Now, Donald, you first."

The boys' father then listened closely to both sides, hearing out each child. Then, after thinking about what they had said, he suggested a solution that would be fair to both, though each would have to concede a little. Both boys then returned to watching television, feeling that their needs had been met, that they had been heard, and that their father's solution, though not totally to their liking, could be lived with.

The boys had been taught to deal with everyday situations in a fair and reasonable manner. Their father had provided not only a solution to the immediate issue, but also a model for future problem solving.

This story, of course, could take place only among the Phalni, the three-foot-high wasplike creatures who live on the planet Trilgon III of the Protus Alpha Star System. Nowhere else within the known universe could it actually happen.

There is a strategy that works with sibling rivalry, however. If followed, it will dramatically reduce the wear and tear on parents and significantly change for the better the actual feelings between brothers and sisters.

The inspiration for this strategy came from my own childhood. I was the middle child between my sisters, Mary, two years younger, and Ellen, two years older. We were fortunate to have two very good, loving parents. I admire and have tried to emulate with my own children much of what my parents did with us. However, in regard to the problem of sibling fighting, my parents didn't exactly have it down to a science.

As adults, my two sisters and I are close, and have been for many years. But as children we could not go anywhere, could not do anything, could not even just be in the same room together without constant bickering, arguing, screaming, case pleading, outraged tantruming. Ellen and I didn't battle that much, but that was only because we were too busy tormenting Mary, the baby of the family, who had the triple disadvantage that she was younger, physically smaller and thinner, and also cried easily.

My clear memory of the incessant bickering that was so much a part of my house when growing up gave me the strong resolve that Mary Alice and I should come up with a better plan for Nick and Margaret. Mary Alice agreed with me, and we made a conscious decision when Margaret and Nick were probably no older than two and four that we would follow three rules in regard to their fighting. I can only say that what we did worked.

1. We would never intervene by taking one side or the other. The one exception was if it seemed that either Nick or Margaret was in real danger of getting hurt.
2. We would *never* listen if they came to us because of an argument. Never. Ever. If we intervened both suffered the consequences, which usually meant being told to stop bickering. If that failed, both were banished to separate places. We paid no attention to who was at fault, and when they would try to plead their cases to us, we absolutely would not listen.
3. We would intervene only when their bickering became too irritating, or if altercations seemed to get out of hand.

The message was clear: the one and only sibling-rivalry crime that is serious enough to get you singled out is when you might potentially injure your sibling.

"You cannot throw the toy truck at your sister. It could hurt her."

"But she kicked me and she messed up my baseball cards."

"You cannot throw toy trucks at your sister."

But injury does not mean pain.

"What is that shrieking?" inquires the children's mother as she comes into the room to see Chucky sitting on his younger sister Jocelyn, slowly twisting her nose.
"Both of you, stop it now, or you go to your rooms."
"But Chucky's twisting my nose."
"Yeah, but Jocelyn threw my tyrannosaurus in the toilet."
"I don't want to hear about it."

Why would she want to?
Not only would Mary Alice and I refuse to listen, but I had a rule that if one of the children told on the other— "Nicky poured his milk down the sink"—I would do nothing, even if the transgression was something for which Nick would normally have been reprimanded. I considered all such information as inadmissible evidence.

Over time, Nick and Margaret basically gave up trying to tell us who started what, whose fault it was, because on those subjects we *never* listened to them. In truth, Nick and Margaret may have fought as much as other children. What was different was the lack of involvement of their parents. Not having to endure that kind of bickering made a huge difference for Mary Alice and me. Being with the two kids was almost always fun.

The truth about sibling fighting is that one can either train one's children to work it out themselves or train them to rely on a parent to work things out for them. Should parents become the resolvers of arguments, they will find that arguments rarely get resolved. Instead, parents will invariably find themselves caught up in ongoing squabbling. All their children will learn is expertise in case pleading.

When parents refuse to get involved, children are left with a choice: somehow work things out or risk parental displeasure.

"You can't watch TV without squabbling? Then nobody watches TV."

Or:

"If you two can't be here in the kitchen without all of that bickering, then I want both of you out of here."

This strategy puts the burden on the children. It eliminates any idea of "If we can't work it out, we'll go to Mommy and Daddy." With parents removed, most of the time children work things out.

Frequently, however, when children are left on their own to work things out, their resolutions are not always what we would have chosen. The basis for their resolution is more often "what I can live with" rather than fairness. Nonetheless, these can be real and necessary compromises and useful lessons for day-to-day living.

"I don't mind Sara taking my clothes without asking and sometimes ruining them, so long as I can hit her and make her cry when she ruins something I really like."

"Yeah, Sherri hits me sometimes. But I get to wear her clothes."

Even when they do not always succeed at finding resolutions, they often learn the general limits beyond which they cannot push each other, which teaches them to avoid the blowups that will bring in their angry parents.

Sibling Rivalry

Perhaps the most important result of my policy is its effect on the feelings between brothers and sisters. Where sibling squabbling pulls a parent into the role of judge and jury, the whole nature of the relationship between the siblings is transformed. Let's say there was an argument between a brother and a sister over who got control of the television. If a parent does not get involved and the argument stays reasonably quiet and nonviolent, then all that is at stake is what TV shows you get to watch.

But if a parent gets involved, everything changes. Now added into the argument is the question of whose side the parent will be on, and this is a very powerful issue for all children. Plainly, it is a direct food call to the baby self. It is so powerful, in fact, that the original issue of getting control of the television pales in comparison. Conflicts between siblings immediately become battles for parental favor. All that remains are two voracious baby selves looking for their next feeding. Dueling baby selves.

"I didn't ever, Mom. He's lying."
"She did, Mom. She took it. She's the one who's lying."

A common phenomenon—it happened with my two sisters and me—is that children who fight bitterly throughout childhood and even genuinely hate each other during those years (at least that is the only feeling they are in touch with) find to their surprise that when they leave their parental home, now with no parents to compete over, they suddenly get along fine. Although all during their childhood the rivalry may have been intense, the genuine ill will that existed between them was simply a direct product of being constantly pitted against one another in the battle for parental favor.

What I am really recommending in regard to sibling bickering is that nobody gets blamed. I am recommending that the question of who was at fault, except where real harm does or could occur, be simply taken out of the equation. And with

Brother and Sister Baby Selves Let Their Father Settle an Argument

its absence, life with more than one child becomes so much more pleasant—for everybody.

Big Bullies, Little Victims?

If brothers and sisters are left to work things out on their own, won't the bigger and older one invariably bully the younger and smaller one, and won't that have a bad effect on the smaller child?

This is a valid concern.

Nine-year-old Isaiah is a lot bigger and stronger than his seven-year-old brother, Joshua. What is to stop Isaiah from bullying Joshua if his parents never intervene except for risk of injury or when the two of them are making too much noise?

"That's it, you two."
"But Isaiah is beating me up."
"I said stop it or you'll go to your rooms."

If that's the deal, why won't Isaiah simply hit Joshua whenever the mood strikes him. Why won't he constantly bully his younger brother? The answer is simple: if parental favor truly is removed as an issue between the two of them, there remains no deep reason for them to dislike each other. This is especially important in regard to Isaiah. Though his younger brother may at times pester him, get into his stuff, one particular scene does not happen. Joshua does not go running to his parent crying "Isaiah hit me," with repercussions for Isaiah. If Isaiah sees instead that Joshua, by virtue of being younger, smaller, and weaker, cannot automatically get his parents on his side, the one great impediment to an older sibling liking a younger one is removed.

Isaiah may sometimes bully Joshua, he may use his superior size as an advantage over his younger brother and even feel good about it. But this also allows him at times to act charitably toward his little brother, even at times to like him.

But what about Joshua? Isn't he the victim? Won't he suffer? Won't he be damaged?

Not really. Joshua will not be completely defenseless. In truth, little ones always have a defense against physical aggression: screaming. A parent will step in to separate the two even though blame may not be doled out. Also, Joshua will get his licks in. If he's like most younger siblings, he will figure out ways to tease and aggravate Isaiah. Even though there may be the risk of getting punched, Joshua will at times attack anyway, quite possibly choosing those times when a parent is handy to run and hide behind.

Still, there will be times that Joshua does get bullied with no recourse for revenge, times that he will suffer at Isaiah's hands and will genuinely resent his older brother. But being bullied is ultimately not a serious problem for Joshua, because of a fact of human nature regularly observed by parents. Little ones tend to idolize, tend to love their big brothers and sisters. Little ones genuinely hate it when they get picked on and they do genuinely suffer, but this doesn't seem to stop them from loving their big brother or sister anyway. They do not seem deterred from going right back to a bigger sibling after an unpleasant incident has ended. This is especially true if there are times when the bigger sibling is nice to his younger brother or sister, the chances for which significantly increase when "Joshua can always get Mom on his side because he's such a baby" is not part of the equation.

Most parents have witnessed the speed with which a younger sibling, recently pummeled or ridiculed into heartbroken despondency, can swiftly recover and seek to reengage.

"Isaiah, will you play a game with me?"

Which, in fact, Isaiah may be disposed to do. Having only minutes before reduced his brother to tears, but having no outstanding grievance against him, Isaiah may at that point feel far more charitable.

But what about verbal abuse? Might it not actually damage their self-esteem?

Brianna, nine, often temperamental, was frequently disposed to taking out her bad moods on her five-year-old sister, Sonya.

"That drawing's awful. You're gonna have to learn to draw. You're so stupid."

And at such times, Sonya, who is described by her mother as the "gentlest little dumpling," would just take it, sitting there saying nothing. But then her lower lip would start to quiver and she would burst into sobs.

"It's so sad when Brianna puts her down like that," Sonya's mother would say. "Sonya really looks up to Brianna. She takes what Brianna says so much to heart."

Does Sonya take it to heart? Does it become a part of her self-image? *I am bad at drawing. I am dumb.*

Unlike teasing that comes from a peer, teasing from a sibling doesn't count. Though initially hurt by their sisters' words, the Sonyas of the world ultimately do learn that what sisters say, even idolized big sisters, is nothing more than attempts to get them upset. They are not statements of true character flaws by a knowing judge, but only aggravating verbal jabs, similar to a pinch or a hair pull, only more clever. Also, in time, the Sonyas do learn to speak up for themselves.

"I am not bad at drawing. You're bad at drawing."

If left on their own, younger siblings also develop a certain toughness, a certain counterpunching ability, that allows them to deal with critical jabs and not always be a victim, to rebound from the *normal* unpleasantness of day-to-day life. This toughness, not taking everything to heart, not taking everything personally, is necessary for dealing with the everyday world. We want to produce children who can stand up for themselves, who in the face of adversity do not crumble in despair. Sonya's mother would want to do all she could to de-

velop this ability in her younger daughter. She would want
Sonya to get such training. And what better training for such
skills than fending off a verbally abusive older sister?

"Sonya, your breath smells."
"Yours smells worse."

If the abuse seems too much, parents can always intervene and separate the two. But maybe in time Sonya learns all
on her own and in her own way to handle her big sister. Two
baby selves toe to toe.

"You're a butt brain."
"*You're* a butt brain."

If Parents Aren't There: A Witnessed Scene and a Question

As I initially worked on this section, outside a motel room in
Michigan where I was staying, three children began playing
shuffleboard—two girls about twelve years old and a nine-
year-old boy, apparently the brother of one of the girls. There
were no parents anywhere in evidence.

"Teach me how to play," said the boy.
"No, watch. You'll learn," said his sister.
"Teach me," said the boy.
"Just watch."
Not satisfied, the boy went over and grabbed one of the
four shuffleboard pucks.
"Fine. We'll play without it. You're such a baby," said his
sister.
The boy took the puck and sat on a low wall nearby. The
girls started to play using the three pucks.
The boy flung the puck in a direction away from the girls.

"You *have* to teach me," he said.

"Just watch and you'll learn," said his sister.

The boy retrieved the puck and threw it toward his sister. "Catch."

He then sat down next to the shuffleboard court and watched the girls play.

I noticed them again maybe ten minutes later. The girls apparently had been playing and the boy watching.

"You said three innings and then it was my turn to play. You played four," said the boy.

"No, we haven't."

"Yes, you have. This is the fourth."

"One was warm up. *This* is the third," said his sister.

The boy, not buying it, leaped up from his chair, took all four of the pucks, and ran away with them shouting, "I'm not giving them back."

The boy then threatened to drop them in the swimming pool.

"You'll get in trouble."

The boy didn't drop the pucks in the pool, but glared at his sister. The girls walked away. The boy, still holding the pucks, watched.

The girls stopped and turned.

"Are you going to give us the pucks?"

"One more inning and that's it," said the boy, flinging the pucks back to them.

What would happen if there had been parents around? I leave the answer to my readers' imaginations.

11

♦♦

At Home and Elsewhere

Bedtime

There's that noise again. It's the thing in the wall. Mommy says it's nothing, but it's not nothing. It's going to get out and kill me. Do you think your body can feel anything when you're dead?

Bedtime is perhaps the number one problem time for the baby self because it requires what the baby self hates above all else, being alone and separated from its parents. Bedtime is not only being alone, but having to be alone in the dark with robbers, monsters, and ghosts.

"And then the giant butterfly flew off to its home in the faraway hills of Nevermore. 'Good-bye,' it called. 'Good-bye, everyone. Good-bye, Silly Billy.' Good night, Becky darling, darlingest. See you in the morning."

"Good night, Mommy. I love you."

"I love you, too, my Becky darling."

"One more hug?"

"One more hug."

"Just one more hug, just one more?"

"Okay, but this is the last hug."

"Please, just one more?"

"No, Becky. It's time to go to sleep."

"Just one more? I won't sleep unless I get another hug."

"All right, but this *is* the last hug."

"Don't leave yet. Sit with me."

Becky's mother finally gets away but not before missing the first five minutes of her favorite show, "Intensive Caring." But still, peace at last.

Shuffle. Shuffle. Shuffle.

"Mommy, I think my eye hurts."

"What do you mean you *think* your eye hurts?"

"I know it does. It hurts. Look at my eye."

"Becky, go to bed."

"But it hurts. I think there's something in it."

"Becky, there's nothing in your eye."

"Ooh! It hurts when I blink."

"If it's still a problem in the morning, I'll look at it."

"But I can't sleep. My eye hurts."

"Becky, why can't you just stay in bed for once like a normal child?"

"I'm not a normal child. I'm a Becky."

"Go to bed, Becky."

"But I'm not a normal child."

How did I get into this?

A common complaint: "I want them in bed at eight o'clock, but sometimes it's almost nine before they're finally in bed for good."

Most people's definition of bedtime is that time when the children are in bed, the lights are out, and all is quiet. Let me propose a different, more useful definition of bedtime that takes into account the reality of the baby self.

Bedtime is the end of all meaningful contact with parents.

"Good night, Mommy. I love you."
"I love you, too, my Becky darling."
"One more hug?"
"One more hug."

And let's say Becky's mother always gives her daughter three one-more-hugs but the third is the last. The third one-more-hug is the end of meaningful contact with her mother.

"Just another hug? Just one more?"
"One more hug." (This is now the third.)
"Please, one more, one more."
"Good night, my Becky."
"Please, just one more."

But Becky's mother has already turned to leave and is now walking out of the room. She does not turn back.

"Just one more. Please, one more."

But Becky is talking to air. Her mother is gone.

"Mommy! MOMMY! I still need another hug so I can go to sleep. MOMMY!"

But Becky's pleas should go unanswered. And if Becky gets out of bed—

"I think my eye hurts."

Or:

"I need a drink of water." (She can't get it herself?)

Or:

"I have to go to the bathroom." (She has to announce it?)

Or:

"I'm worried about what Kimmy is going to say to me to-morrow in school." (Should have thought of that earlier.)

Regardless, what Becky now needs to see is that nurturing Mommy has been replaced by Robot Mommy. She is benign and watchful and there for true emergencies such as significant quantities of blood, or thick black smoke, or a robber whom Becky can actually produce. But otherwise, Mommy is completely unresponsive except for an occasional flat-toned, unemotional:

"Good night, Becky."
"But it hurts. I can't sleep."
"Good night, Becky."

Children have the ability to fall asleep on their own, although not all kids have the same sleep patterns. Some fall asleep quickly. Some fidget and stay awake longer or may need to read or play quietly on their own before they finally fall asleep. Those who take longer should be allowed to do that, as long as they do it quietly, on their own, separate from

parents and not bothering anybody. Parents should only intervene if children are playing too loudly or are disturbing siblings.

Ultimately, parents have to make a decision. Do I want
my child to learn to fall asleep on her own or do I want her to
depend on my being there in order to fall asleep?

Of course, parents want to be available when worries and
fears out of the ordinary come up, such as a particularly scary
movie, a big kid threatening to beat up their child in school,
the family dog loose on the streets and almost hit by a car. You
want to reassure children about monsters, witches, and robbers.

*If I lie real still maybe the monster won't know I'm here so
then it won't kill me.*

"There are no monsters. No witches. No ghosts. Just us
here to protect you."

But over time, beyond anything parents might say, there is
only one true reassurance. They fall asleep and they wake up
the next morning and the monster didn't kill them after all.

*I was lucky. But tonight—he's probably mad because I
fooled him last night—he really will kill me.*

But nights go by and the monster never comes. The night-
time anxieties never do totally leave—even into adult life—
but children can learn, if their parents will just stay out of the
way, that sleep does come. The worries may be there, but they
are part of life, no big deal. If bedtime is defined as the end
of meaningful interaction with parents, then that's what it
means. "Evelyn, turn out your light" is not in the picture.
"Bedtime" must remain the time after which they're alone—
all alone.

The Baby Self Goes to Bed

Getting Up and Out in the Morning

I can't stand it. By 7:50 when I finally get the kids out the door, I'm a nervous wreck. Robby has made dawdling into an art form. I keep coming into his room, and if possible, he is more undressed each time, lying on the floor playing with his stupid cars. Not as if we have to be out of the house in ten minutes. He's, like, on the moon.

And with Tatiana, every morning is a scream-a-thon. She has a fit over everything. She can't find her underpants. Her shirt has a spot on it. Her toast is too dark. By the time she leaves I want to strangle her.

Getting up and out, actually leaving the house in the morning, goes directly against all that the baby self stands for, and it wants none of it. It is a time of separation from home and parent, plus it demands that the baby self give way to the mature self in order to head out into the world and deal with all the stresses out there.

No, thank you. The baby self will do all it can to dawdle and cling. It will invent endless problems and argue over anything and everything.

"But why can't I bring my basketball to school?"

Yet there is hope. For parents who are totally exhausted by mornings, there is a strategy that can avoid most of the aggravation.

Nick and Margaret trained me about mornings. They demonstrated repeatedly that their progress in getting up and dressed was *inversely* proportional to how much I tried to push them forward. My presence, let alone my nagging—"Come on, Nick, get your shirt on"—only seemed to inspire dawdling. In the morning, the more you try to move them forward the less you get anywhere, because all the baby self wants to do is to grab hold of you and cling.

In the end I learned to be elsewhere, usually in the kitchen fixing breakfast. Rather than go to their rooms, I would call to them from a distance. (Where was Mary Alice? She says it was usually *she*, not I, who got them up and made sure they ate something for breakfast.)

"Getting dressed? Ten minutes until we leave."

And usually they would be ready on time. The secret of mornings is not to try very hard. You want to keep interaction at an absolute minimum unless it's pleasant stuff that is not trying to accomplish anything. In the morning, nagging just is not the way to go. It only ensures that they will dawdle and argue and that you will become infuriated.

A good procedure for mornings is as follows:

1. Make sure they are awake: "Morning, time to get up."
2. Periodically, but from a distance, let them know that time is passing. "It's 7:25. Half an hour before it's time to go." (It doesn't matter if they completely understand time. The communication simply says there's something out there called time and it's moving right along, with or without you.)
3. Do nothing else until ten minutes before it is time for them to leave. At which point, regardless of what stage they are in—even lying totally naked on their backs counting spots on the ceiling—call to them, "Five minutes!" (You are reserving an extra five minutes for step 4.)
4. If the five minutes is up and they have failed to appear, you go to where they are, and dress them swiftly and not especially lovingly. (It's essential that you allow enough time at the end to avoid everyone's running late.) Get what they need for school, give them some kind of portable breakfast snack if they have failed to eat breakfast, and get them out the door.

In effect, this procedure says to children: you *can* dawdle the whole morning if you wish, but, at the end, you will be dressed and out the door. You can have me do it, or you can do it yourself. It's your choice.

Most children, given this choice, usually dress themselves and eat breakfast in the morning without any nagging from you. The true dawdlers will probably still do it at the last minute, but they'll do it because they know that when you say "Five Minutes!" they have five minutes to either dress themselves or have you take over.

In the mornings, less is definitely the way to go.

The Baby Self Gets Ready for School

I Don't Know Where My Shoes Are

"Mom, I don't know where my shoes are."

"Jeremy, we're leaving in twenty minutes."

"Well, I don't know where my shoes are."

"Did you look for them?"

"Yeah. I can't find them."

"Where is the last place you left them?"

"I don't know. I don't remember. I don't know where they are."

"Well, think, Jeremy."

"I can't think. You're yelling at me. I don't know where they are."

"Jeremy, I've had it with you. I have to get ready to go. I don't want to have to be looking for your shoes."

"Well, I don't know where they are."

Jeremy's mother has a choice. She can engage and go look for Jeremy's shoes or, an often wiser alternative, she can back off.

"Mom, I don't know where my shoes are."
"Gosh, that's a problem." (For him, not me.)
"But I can't find my shoes."
"I guess you'll have to look more."
"I did. I can't find them."
"Gosh, I don't know what to tell you."
"But I can't find my shoes."
"I hope you find them before it's time to go."
"I can't find my shoes."

At that point Jeremy's mother should just continue about her business. If Jeremy still hasn't found his shoes just before it is time to go, then she will have to look for them. But surprisingly often, if his mother shows absolutely no interest in what should be Jeremy's job, Jeremy finds his shoes all on his own.

"I found them. They were under my bed."
"Good for you, Jeremy."

In the Car

"Mom, Carlton keeps touching my pants."
"Carlton, stop touching your sister's pants."
"Well, she kicked my shoe."
"Yvette, stop kicking your brother's shoe."
"But he won't stop touching my pants."
"Carlton, stop touching your sister's pants, now!"
"I won't stop unless Yvette stops kicking my shoe."
"Okay, on the count of three both of you stop. One. Two. Three."

"Carlton cheated. He did a touch after the three."

"You little brat, Yvette."

"Mom, Carlton punched me hard on the arm."

As I've mentioned, being in the car with your children takes away your number one weapon—separation, either of siblings or parent and child. In this respect, you're stuck. And, of course, they know this.

"Okay, Trish, I'm stopping at the next gas station and getting out. You will have to drive yourself and Bobby the rest of the way. I'm taking a cab."

"But I'm only six."

"You should have thought of that before you kept fighting after I told you to stop, shouldn't you? Next time maybe you'll listen to Mommy."

One child in a car is rarely a problem. But more than one can be tough. There are fewer problems when they are of an age that requires car seats. But even this does not always work.

"Mom, Krista's blowing on my hair."

If you are on top of your game, preemptive strikes often work.

"Okay, I want each of you to tell me about three things that happened in your day."

"Let's do the license plate game, but today we'll see who's the first person to get twenty nines . . . I just got two."

"No fair, you didn't say start."

"I got three."

Overall, however, the best rule as always is to respond as little as possible to the fussing.

"Dad, Bethany is hogging the space."
"I am not. Ricky is too fat."
"Dad, Bethany said I was fat."
"You are, you little crybaby."
"I am not. You're a crybaby."
"Well, if I'm a crybaby, how come you're the one who's crying?"
"I'm not crying."

An occasional "Will you two please stop?" may momentarily slow them down. But beyond that, less is best. If they know that, overall, their bickering will not pull you into their squabbles, in the car, as everywhere else, you will get less of it.

But there can be times where the fighting is just too awful, or may even threaten your ability to drive safely. In such instances many parents learn to simply pull over to the side of the road and sit.

"We are not going anywhere until all of you stop it."

In the vast majority of instances, and after a brief period of mandatory fussing, they do stop. For long car rides, it is always advisable to bring along as much portable entertainment as possible. It is an excellent time for activity books. And if there ever were a place in which handheld video games were a blessing, it is long car rides.

However, the best solution of all to fussing in the car is as it always has been: getting there.

Meal Time

Mary Alice's and my own work schedules rarely allowed for regular, whole-family-sitting-down-to-supper meals. A lot of my eating was done sitting in front of the television, a practice of which I am personally quite fond. So I am not someone to write of the sacredness of family meals. But for many families, meals can be a special time shared and enjoyed by everyone. And for families who eat together, meals should never have to be an ordeal to get through.

At supper seven-year-old Lynnette kept up a stream of aggravating behavior.

"Why can't we ever have anything I like? Ooh, this is disgusting. Ooh, it's gross."

"If you don't like it, you don't have to eat it," said her mother.

"Keep your hands away from my plate," said Lynnette, smacking her younger brother hard on his hand, which was nowhere near her at all.

"Don't hit Lyle. He wasn't doing anything," said her father. Whereupon Lynnette started kicking the underside of the table.

"Stop kicking the table," said her mother.

Whereupon Lynnette started rocking back in her chair. "Well, I hate my supper. I hate it. It's disgusting. Disgusting."

Separation is in order if a given family member is making the meal significantly unpleasant for others. If someone is being obnoxious and seems intent on continuing to be obnoxious, there is no point in their being at the table. They are not harmed by eating elsewhere or at another time.

"Good-bye, Lynnette."
"No. I'm not doing anything."
"Good-bye, Lynnette."

But remember the rule for separation. If she is banished she is welcome back at any time, as long as she behaves. If family meals are pleasant, then the absented child will want to return unless she is in a really bad or especially squirmy mood. In which case she might not want to return, nor would you want her back.

There are some basic guidelines that you can follow for meals:

1. Decide what level of meal chaos is acceptable to you. Remember, if you are going to have meals with human children, some imperfect behavior will occur.

   "Taylor, when you eat you look just like a little pig."
   "At least I don't drool like you do."

2. Ignore what falls within your acceptable limits of fussing or silliness. Do not constantly correct.

   "Kayla, please do not rock back on the legs of the chair."

   "Kayla, elbows off the table."

   "Kayla, how are you supposed to hold your fork?

3. If a child is to the point where she is spoiling everyone's meal, then that child should be banished until she can return and be reasonably pleasant. Family meals are supposed to be a pleasant time, with or temporarily without a given family member.

"Good-bye, Edward."

"But I'm the father! I'm not supposed to be banished."

"Good-bye, Edward."

"Wait a minute. Dr. Wolf didn't mean adults, too."

"Good-bye, Edward."

"Go for it, Mom."

"He didn't mean adults, Ruth."

Picky Eaters

All that parents ask is that each day their children funnel into their bodies an adequate amount of reasonably nutritious food. It's not asking a lot, but trying to get your children to eat what you think they should eat can drive you crazy.

"Conrad, will you please stop playing with your food and eat?"

"But I'm not hungry, and besides the skin on this piece of chicken is gross."

"Well, I'll cut it off."

"No. The gross skin has already touched the chicken."

In any given instance, pressuring children to eat might work. But overall, each time you try adds to the potential of future trouble. They learn that they can use eating as a means of entry into potential parent-baiting, and they will.

"Just eat those eight beans for me."

"It will make you happy?"

"Yes, it will make me happy."

"Then I won't."

"You said I could have dessert if I eat eight green beans. How about if I eat six?"

"Eight."
"Seven?"

It becomes a power struggle and, as I have mentioned, there are two areas where parents absolutely do not want to get into any kinds of power struggles with their children—eating and matters of the toilet. These battles inevitably bring emotional issues into areas where they do not belong. We want eating to be emotion-free. We do not want to contaminate it with battles over control.

With children who never seem to eat much, simply have regular meals and make the food available. If they pick at their food instead of eating, limit meal time. When meal time is over, they can leave the table. Forget about their sitting at the table until they eat what you consider a sufficient amount.

You need to set up a standard policy for picky eaters. Is their food still available to them after they leave the table? Are they allowed to have an alternative—a peanut butter sandwich or cereal—if they want it? Under what conditions can they have dessert? The policy is your choice, and any policy is okay because it's your choice, it's standard, it doesn't change, and there will never be any negotiating about it.

However, making special and different meals is not a good policy. It only invites children to continue seeking special food treatment.

If you're worried about the effect of their eating habits on their health, ask their doctor. If there is a problem, their doctor will let you know. Very few children living in homes where there is an adequate supply of food are undernourished. The vast majority of children eat enough for their own nutritional purposes.

Lying

"Bobo!"

"What?"

"Did you spill orange juice and make this mess on the kitchen floor?"

"No."

"Bobo, I know it was you. Tracy and Sam have been with me since I was last in the kitchen and it didn't spill itself."

"It wasn't me. I didn't spill the orange juice."

"Don't lie to me, Bobo."

"I'm not lying. Somebody else did it. I don't know who. I didn't do it, Mom. Honest." Bobo, who was lying through his teeth, sounded very sincere.

"I'm going to give you one more chance, and I want you to tell me the truth. Did you spill the orange juice?"

"No, Mom. I didn't."

"I know you're lying, Bobo."

"I'm not, Mom. I'm not. I'm not lying."

It is in the nature of children to lie. It is what they do when confronted about an act they fear might bring parental wrath or nasty consequences.

"Jason, was it you who left the water running in the sink?"
"No."

"Anna Lee, did you wash your hands?"
"Yes."

"Sissy, did you eat all the chocolate macadamia nut cookies?"
"No, I just ate one."

Children often lie even when there is nothing that they are going to be blamed for. Just the slightest possibility of blame can induce them to lie.

"Sondra, were you just in your room?"
"No." But she was.
"Oh, I just wondered if I left my knitting in there."
"No, it's not in my room. Actually I *was* just there."

What was Sondra afraid of? Probably she wasn't even sure. Just the phrasing of the question made her wary.

Children lie where it is bizarrely obvious that they are lying.

"Holden, did you take Nicholas's purple troll?"
"No."
"What is that?"
"I don't know," Holden replies while clutching the purple troll in his right hand.

Children lie as an immediate way to deflect blame, because they don't like to be blamed. It doesn't seem to matter whether parents are harsh and nasty or loving and gentle. The fear of blame seems universally lodged in children's heads, and to escape, they lie. Being totally honest is not easy for them (or for the rest of us, for that matter).

"Sissy, did you eat all the chocolate macadamia nut cookies?"
"Yes, I did. I know I wasn't supposed to. But they were just so good I couldn't stop myself. So I ate them all."

Now we're back with the wasplike Phalni on Trilgon III of the Protus Alpha Star System. Human children don't reply in this way. The answer leaves them feeling too open to blame. In her head, Sissy winces at her mother's imagined blaming voice.

"You ate ALL of them? Sissy, how could you? That is disgraceful! You're in big trouble now."

So she lies instead.
So what should parents do about lying?

"Bobo!"
"What?"
"Bobo, would you please clean up this orange juice."
"I didn't spill it."
"Bobo, would you please clean up the orange juice."
Notice there is no mention of Bobo's denial.
"But I didn't spill it."
"Bobo, just clean up the orange juice."

Maybe Bobo's mother can get him to clean up the orange juice and maybe she cannot. But it's the cleanup, not the lying, on which Bobo's mother chooses to focus. No time is spent on establishing whether Bobo spilled the orange juice or not, which his mother knows he did, and which Bobo knows his mother knows. Parents can focus on the lying, or they can focus on the issue that provoked the lying—cleaning up the mess, turning off faucets, washing hands before dinner.
I recommend the latter course.

"Jason, was it you who left the water running in the sink?"
"No."
"Well, I had to turn it off. It wastes water. Try to remember to turn it off after you use the sink."

"Anna Lee, did you wash your hands?"

"Yes."

"I don't think so. Go in and wash them, now."

"Sissy, did you eat all the chocolate macadamia nut cookies?"

"I just ate one."

"Sissy, I told you not to eat all the cookies. I asked you not to. I just don't think I can leave bags of cookies around anymore."

You can pick up on the lying if you want. But the truth is that to do so leads nowhere other than to not-useful places and away from whatever was the real issue at hand.

Teaching Honesty

But you can't just ignore the lying. Lying is bad. How will children learn not to lie? How will they learn to be honest?

What are the main parenting ingredients that produce honest kids?

1. Deal with your child honestly. This is by far the most important.
2. Act honestly in your dealings with others. It does set an example for your child.
3. Nurture your child.
4. Set limits and make appropriate demands in the course of child raising.
5. Do not act toward your child in an overly harsh manner.

The last three recommendations would seem to have little to do with honesty. But they do, because to be honest you have to be able to own up to your mistakes, and you have to trust that you can survive in the world without having to be dishonest. To own up to mistakes and to be honest requires that you feel good about yourself and your ability to survive in the world. The last three recommendations produce that confidence.

Noticeably absent from this list is lecturing your child that lying is bad. Actually, this does have some effect, but its role is really minor. As any parent knows, castigating and perhaps punishing children for lying has zero effect on whether they will or will not lie again. Mainly, they just become more careful about not being caught. They become better liars.

Storytelling

Nate to a friend, overheard by his mother:

"So last weekend we went to visit my grandfather. He is very rich. He lives in a mansion and he has lots of horses and whenever we go there, I get to ride his horses. If you don't believe me, see this bruise on my arm? That's how I got the bruise. Falling off one of his horses. I'm not a very good horse rider yet, but I'm getting to be."

Not a word of truth in that story, but such storytelling is an altogether different species from lying. Lying is to escape blame. Storytelling is to increase one's status in the eyes of others. It is very normal and it is something that children usually outgrow, especially as their friends increasingly become doubters.

"You're so full of bull, Nate."

Nate's parents need not interfere because experience will teach Nate to curb his storytelling. However, sometimes extensive storytelling can be a warning sign that a particular child may lack confidence, and parents should be watchful for such signs. But the bottom line is that storytelling, even a lot of storytelling, falls well within the norms of childhood.

But there can be *unintended* ramifications of storytelling.

"I've been embarrassed to say anything, but I really do feel so badly about you and Susanna getting a divorce. I've always thought of you two as such a perfect couple."

"Getting a *what?*"

"Well, yes, Booker has been telling everyone in school. I know it must be very hard for him."

Booker hadn't thought out the effect that his story would have on others.

"I was only joking, Dad. They thought I was serious."

But Booker had been serious, liking the added drama and focus on him. In such cases parents want to intervene.

"Booker, saying that your mother and I are getting a divorce was not good. Now lots of people think we are getting a divorce, and it's embarrassing to me and your mother since it's not true."

The message: storytelling can have unintended consequences, so you do have to watch what you say.

Picking Up Rooms

"Mommy, I can't find Jenny."

"Davis, what do you mean you can't find Jenny? I thought she was in your room with you."

"She is, but I can't find her."

"Not again."

And then Davis and his mother, as they had done many times in the past, entered Davis's room and waded through the accumulated waist-high jumble of toys, clothes, dirty dishes, etc., and finally did find Davis's four-year-old sister, Jenny, submerged in the sea of stuff, happily playing with the broken action figure Davis had gotten three Christmases ago.

"How many times do I have to tell you to wear your beeper when you play in Davis's room?" said her angry mother.

"I'm sorry, Mommy," said Jenny.

In regard to rooms, I offer the following suggestions:

1. If you want to have children who will pick up their rooms on a day-to-day basis, you have to set a regular time for them to do so, best is just before bed. This way messes do not accumulate too much. With parental diligence, the habit of picking up one's room on a regular basis should kick in. However, this routine has a much better chance of success if you start when they are young.
2. What many parents have learned to do, which also seems to work, is to pick a weekly time, usually a Saturday or a Sunday morning. Their child is not allowed to do anything else until the room is picked up.
3. A last piece of advice is that for very big messes, the really daunting tasks, it is a good idea to help them do it, especially with younger children. Just make sure that you are not doing all of it.

Chores

Eighty-seven-year-old Clem "Turkey Legs" Haskins on kids today:

"When I was a kid I used to get up at four in the morning every day and go out and milk the cows. Didn't matter if it was twenty degrees below zero, I had to do it. Kids today, you can't tell them to do *nothing*.

"Did I ever tell you the story about me and "Pig Eyes" Burkett and the time he fell in the river? I did tell it to you, huh?"

Clem Haskins milked the cows out of necessity. His parents were already busy doing their chores. If he didn't milk the cows, they would go without being milked. But in today's homes, necessity is less clear.

"Jasmine, if you don't pick up your room, it will turn into a pigsty."

But unless the Board of Health actually shuts down Jasmine's bedroom, she can live very happily amidst her jungle of accumulated stuff.

My only point: the nature of necessity has changed. All kinds of electrical appliances exist that did not in Clem Haskins's childhood. Furthermore, as we've discussed, parents today have less time to follow through on demands for chores to be done, and less time to be there to oversee that they are done, both critical requirements for getting compliance. Therefore, chores simply are not going to be completed as diligently as in the past.

But if they don't regularly do chores as kids won't they grow up to be lazy good-for-nothings?

So long as demands are made regularly, even though compliance may fall short of what most parents wish, children do mature and the vast majority do become hard-working adults.

Schoolwork

If there is one area that I would recommend parents use their limited time and energy to get their children to do what they do not feel like doing, it is homework. I recommend homework as a top priority because, after all, it is an investment in your children's future.

But homework is a problem *by definition,* since home is where the baby self wants to come out and stay out. Homework requires that at least for a certain amount of time a child has to switch back into the mature-self mode. He would rather not.

"Oh, please? Can I do my homework now? Please? Can I? Please?"

Only from children with very high fevers.

"I don't have a high fever. I do love doing homework. I do. Especially book reports. I love book reports, don't I, Mommy?"

"Yes, you do, pumpkin."

It's true. Some children do their homework regularly and put good effort into it, though they do not necessarily enjoy it. But many do not, and, for whatever reason, this is more true of boys than of girls.

With children who regularly and adequately do their homework, it is still good to be involved, to see what they are doing. Offer help where needed or asked for, and praise them when they clearly have put time and effort into what they have done.

With children who are not so good about doing homework, I have one basic suggestion. Set designated homework times. When should these be? School nights—Monday through Thursday and Sunday nights—are probably best. Whether it's after school, after supper, or before bed probably doesn't matter as much as finding a time slot that is convenient for you and acceptable to your child. A regular time each day is best, but it does not have to be the same time every day. For example, if a special TV show is on, or a grandparent comes over for a visit, then the homework time can be shifted. *Shifted*, not skipped.

They should do their homework in a "public" room in the house, one where you can keep an eye on them. Kitchens are good, but their own rooms are not good. Too many distractions in there. Public rooms may have more noise and more occasional family commotion, but they really work best.

The requirements for these homework times are as follows:

1. A parent is present, not necessarily in the room, but at least nearby.
2. The only thing a child is allowed to do is schoolwork. Nothing else may be done. No games, no TV, no phone calls, nothing except schoolwork. You cannot *make* a child do schoolwork. But it is much easier to induce the effort if they are not allowed to do anything else.
3. The homework time should be for a finite period for each session, getting progressively longer as a child gets older. It must be a realistic appraisal of the time necessary to complete the work, but it should not be too long, or open-ended, thus avoiding the torturous case of whole evenings spent doing what should have taken half an hour.

201

I tell him that the sooner he's finished, the sooner he'll get to do what he wants. But he just goes on and on with his fussing and his dawdling—until finally it's done. If it gets done. And I'm totally exhausted.

But what if homework time is over, and the work is not done? They are then free to do what they want. That is the deal.

But what if they do absolutely nothing the whole time?

The homework period is over. The homework did not get done. They, like you, will not be too happy about this. It will provide some motivation for getting it done the next time. Children do not like going to school with incomplete homework. But, of course, such motivation is no guarantee.

There can be exceptions to the rule about having a set amount of time for homework. This would be where a clearly more time-consuming project needs to be done (though, if possible, it should be spread over multiple homework times.) But basically the length of the homework time should be set and remain the same.

The other main advantage of having a finite homework period is that it truly is best for teaching children to use their time efficiently. The whole point of this method is that you are gradually training your child to be able to get work done. At first they may spend much time fussing, dawdling, fidgeting, even just staring into space. But gradually, if they know that there's nothing they can do to escape this period for homework and they are not allowed to do anything else, and if this period keeps coming back day after unrelenting day, then slowly, painfully, with regular backsliding, their efficiency will increase.

They are sitting there. They are expected to do their

homework. They want to do their homework. There is nothing else they are allowed to do. They know that this time will not go on forever. It has a definite, not-so-far-off-in-the-future end. They learn to muster their energy, to rein in all of those forces inside them that scream against focusing and doing work, and for this finite period of time they actually focus and do their work. Most will never use the time with one hundred percent efficiency, but if you end up getting twenty-three minutes of real work in a thirty-minute period, you are doing well.

You do not always have to be right there with them. But especially with younger children, you may need to be present to help. The problem, of course, is that they don't just happily sit there doing the work, attentively responding to your corrections and suggestions.

"No, sweetheart, you're still getting your *d*s and *b*s backward. See, this is the *d* and this is the *b*."

"I don't care. I don't care about *d*s and *b*s. I'm too tired. I'm too tired."

"I know this is hard for you, but you're going to have to learn to do them right."

"But I don't care. I'm too tired. I am."

"But we can't just stop now. We've only been working for ten minutes."

"But I *am* too tired. I can't do this. I hate school. Why can't I stay home tomorrow? I never get to stay home. Why? Why can't I stay home tomorrow? Why not?"

Or, worst of all, they have done work but you feel that it is done incorrectly, or not well enough, or too sloppily, and needs to be done over.

"I'm sorry, Cyrus, this is just not neat enough."

"This *is* neat. This is the way Miss Tuttwelier says to do it. You don't know. This is fine. I don't have to do it again."

Fortunately, the same basic technique for getting kids to do what they do not feel like doing applies here as well: make the demand.

"No, you have to practice the *ds* and *bs.*"

"No, this needs to be done over again—neater."

And if they fuss, *immediately* disengage and quietly wait. Do not pick up on any of their fussing.

"But I can't do it. It's stupid. I hate school. I hate you. I hate this house. I hate Grandma and Pop Pop."

Whatever.

As soon as they start to fuss, disengage and wait. If you can, picture sitting in a chair leaning forward, being involved with what is going on, and then sitting back in the chair, relaxed, waiting, absolutely not picking up on what they say.

When you're ready to continue working, I'm available. I'm here.

If they are really obnoxious you can leave.

"Let me know when you are ready to continue."

And at the end of the homework time, no matter how little may have been accomplished, no matter how much fussing might have gone on:

"Okay, homework time is over."

Negative comments add little.

"Well, we certainly didn't get much done today. I hope tomorrow we'll do better."

What they really need is encouragement for what they do get done, plus the understanding that homework time will *never* go away. It will be there tomorrow and forever.

"I'm not doing my homework ever again. I'm not. I don't care. I'll be a bum like Uncle Danny and live on fake accident claims. I'm not doing homework again. Ever."

But they will. Because all children want to do well in school. All children want to hand in completed and well-done homework. The motivation is always there. Children do not fail because of a lack of motivation. It is just that many simply do not have the self-discipline to do it, and they lack the skills, either intellectual, emotional, organizational, or some combination of the three. These children do not need more motivation. They need help in building skills and compensating for those in which they are weak.

I am not a believer in rewards or punishments for doing schoolwork. For short periods of time they can be effective, but rewards such as an allowance based on grades, or a bike, or a trip to Disney World, or punishments such as no dance lessons for two months do not work over time. If anything, rewards and punishment get in the way of a child's developing any real self-discipline for schoolwork. They supply an *external,* added motivation that *temporarily* may allow children to push through their normal disinclination to do homework. But these rewards or punishments do nothing in developing the internal self-discipline, the *habit* of doing good schoolwork.

Electronics

More from eighty-seven-year-old Clem "Turkey Legs" Haskins reflecting on kids today:

"When I was a kid we used to go outside in any kind of weather and I remember me and Puggy and Rooster Billy (that's what we called him 'cause he always had a comb). We would play for hours even after it got dark, and we'd just have a couple of sticks and some rocks and what we could do with those sticks and rocks you would not believe. Kids today. I tell ya. TV. Them computers. Video games. I don't know what the world's coming to."

The world of electronics—TV, computers, video games, the Internet—has and will continue to change forever forward the world that used to be. Because of this expansion of the electronic world, kids today interact less with the real world than they used to and more with the images and sounds provided by that alternative universe. Good or bad, the electronic universe exists, it is not going to go away, and it has great influence on our children's lives.

You cannot and do not want to fully protect a child from that world. It's too much a part of their future and what they must know and learn to deal with. But there is also no question that the electronic world brings with it very real problems.

One obvious one is the content. Much of what exists in the electronic world is laced with sex, depictions of violence, and wrongful ideas. What's a parent to do? With younger children—since it usually is you who picks and sets up what they watch—monitoring is not very difficult.

"Mommy, will you put on *Bloody Murder at Christmas* for me?"
"No."

But as they get older, controlling what they watch is far more difficult. First, how do you know if what they are watching is harmful or not? One obvious solution is to watch what they watch and see if you are comfortable with it. But not all parents have the time or inclination to do this. Nowadays most TV shows, video games, movies, and Web sites do have some kind of rating as to whether they are appropriate for children or not. There also are some monitors built into the systems themselves that let parents give access only to child-appropriate material. These can be helpful.

Ideally parents can watch what their kids watch, participate in what their children do, and discuss with their kids what may seem troubling. But the truth is that if children are going to have access to the electronic world, full monitoring of what they see is more than what most parents are willing to put in the time and effort to achieve.

Fortunately, beyond monitoring parents have a far more important control as to the possible negative effects that the electronic media may have on their children. The greatest protection parents offer from *outside* influences comes from what they put *inside* their children, from the moral framework they give them through which to view the world. Parents teach this not so much by words, but by how they live. Is their behavior toward their children and toward others guided by moral principles, or not?

I am an eight-year-old boy and watch professional wrestlers act crudely toward women. My father regularly calls me "stupid" whenever I do something wrong, which I hate for him to do. And he regularly does the same with my mother and often talks badly of others, so I don't really have anything inside of me to counteract what I see the pro wrestlers do. "Cool," I think, and then I do the same at recess the next day.

I may get in trouble, but this won't be enough, because there isn't anything *inside* me, put there by my parents.

"It's that pro wrestling," says my mother after grounding me for the week.

Conversely, if my parents have always been respectful of my feelings, and show that same respect in dealing with others, I still may enjoy the crudeness of the pro wrestlers, but I also have a very definite sense that this is not in keeping with how I feel people should be treated. I find the crudeness funny but am far less likely to behave similarly in the real world.

There is another, more subtle problem with parents being too focused on the bad content of media. This concern about protecting children can get in the way of a very different and ultimately more moral focus. The worst that is going on in the world is not the immoral sex and violence in the electronic media. The worst is that there are still many, many people in the world who suffer and many who still do terrible violence to others. Do we worry too much about protecting our kids from exposure to what is bad in the media at the expense of exposing them to the real pain and suffering that is very much out there in the world in which they will soon be citizens? Instead of worrying quite so much about the sex and violence on TV, parents might also want to make sure that their children are made aware that there are many people in the world who are far less fortunate than they.

Separate from its content, there is another problem with the world of electronics. For children, the electronic world can be a very passive one. It supplies the action. There is little that one initiates on one's own. Even with video games you mainly react, not initiate.

"What is it doctor? You have to tell us."
"I'm sorry, Mrs. Perkins. I can't completely explain it but

your Clement's skeletal structure and internal organs seem to be dissolving."

"He's turning into a blob, isn't he, doctor? You can tell me."

"Well, not exactly. A blob with fingers, eyes, a mouth, and ears."

"Oh my God, he'll look just like his father."

Is this to be the next evolutionary step of the human race?

Far too often the world of electronics asks little from a child. Parents know well that after a full day of TV and video games, they are going to have one crabby, restless, slightly depressed child. On the other hand, after a day where children actually *do* something they seem a lot happier. Doing—interacting—exercises not just their bodies but their minds as well.

What is the best of all solutions to the problems inherent in the electronic world? Limit the amount of time that they are plugged in.

"William, you have to turn off the Actavision and come to supper."

"NOOOO!" screamed William, the pupils in his eyes tiny dots, his mouth contorted into a hideous snarl. "NOOOO!"

You can pull the plug.

"William, I have decided that from now on you may have one hour—total—of electronics a day, and that's it. That means *combined*—video games, TV, fun time on the Internet."

"But, Mom!"

And William's mother, to the absolute horror of her son, stuck with her decision. Unfortunately, William, now mostly deprived of what were the main shared interests of his peers, gradually became less and less popular, until he was completely friendless. And not only that, but William, now seriously deprived of the greatest joy in his life, and friendless as well, began to whither away, never smiling, losing weight, spending most of his time quietly whimpering in a corner. Fortunately, the Protective Services people were alerted and William, just in time, was placed in a foster home where a healthy dose of unlimited electronic access restored his strength and natural, bubbly good nature.

For their own benefit, electronic access can and should be denied for significant parts of a child's day at home. But once the TV is off and Internet access is denied, then what?

In today's world, available time has replaced sex and money as the most hoarded of commodities by parents. We do have only a certain amount of time to give. But without the electronic world, your kids will turn to you.

"Mom, I'm bored. Can you do something with me? I'm so bored. I'm bored. I'm bored. I'm bored."

"Gosh, Ethan, have you already gotten bored with the new video game we got you, Lightning Strike III? Or isn't Death Rangers on now? Or how about that Carla Towson show where they humiliate emotionally vulnerable people? You always enjoy that one. You don't need me when there are so many wonderful alternatives."

"Cool, Mom. I hadn't thought of those. What was I thinking? I'll see you in four hours. Love you."

It is, after all, the world's greatest baby-sitter. But with electronic access denied, you do not always have to fill in the gap. As discussed earlier, left to fend for themselves, ultimately they do learn how to fill time all on their own. And that is the whole point. They are the better for it.

When Nothing Works

Sometimes, no matter what you do, nothing works. Parenting disasters are an inevitable part of having children. Sometimes, the kids are a disaster. Sometimes we are a disaster (just ask my children about the latter). The best things about such times is that they end.

Friedrich was playing miniature golf with his younger sister, Maya, and his dad. He wasn't doing too well. He kept missing easy putts and quickly his score was much higher than Maya's. He was getting more and more frustrated, madder and madder until he lost his temper. No longer caring about his own score, he began trying to knock his sister's ball away from the hole.

"Dad, Friedrich's trying to hit my ball and mess up my game."

"Friedrich, this is not croquet," said his father.

"It is if I want it to be. I hate miniature golf. I want to go home. I didn't want to come."

"Your sister and I are going to finish our round." (They still had eight holes to go.)

Friedrich kept aiming at his sister's ball until he finally hit his target and knocked Maya's ball away from where it had been.

"Dad, he's ruining my game," screamed Maya.

"Friedrich, you can't always win."

"I want to go home. This is so boring. Only dorks play miniature golf. I want to go home." And Friedrich started smashing his putter hard into the dirt.

"Don't do that, Friedrich. You might break the club."

"I don't care. I want to go home."

"Well, you're going to have to wait until me and Maya are done. It's not fair to Maya."

"It's not fair to me. I hate this #!%$! place."

"Watch your mouth, Friedrich."

"What the #!%$! are you going to do to me? I want to go home."

I use this example because it's a tough one. Friedrich is breaking about five rules simultaneously—potentially damaging property (a golf club), swearing, being a bad sport, interfering with another individual's right to have a good time—and all of this in public.

I have no easy answer for this one. The basic rule—which always applies—is that Friedrich's father wants to disengage—as best as he can, and as quickly as he can. Also, as discussed, one does not want to let a tantrum force you to go home because it gives too much power to the tantrum thrower and in this case, is unfair to Maya.

However, in tough situations like this, this strategy may not work. Friedrich may continue his tantrum and may continue it in a way that makes it impossible for Maya and her father to continue.

"I'm not going to wait until you and Maya finish. I hate this #!%$! place. I hate it."

And again Friedrich slams his golf club into the dirt.

Unfortunately, Friedrich's father can no longer ignore his son. He can't allow Friedrich to continue to possibly damage property that is not theirs, nor is it fair to the other people playing there to have to hear the swearing continue unabated.

Sometimes one does not have a winnable hand. And in reality, many parents might have lost *their* temper by this point.

"That's it. We're leaving. Get in the car," says Friedrich's father, roughly grabbing his son by the arm.

"Don't you #%!$ touch me."

"It's not fair. I want to finish our game. It's not fair. I don't want to go to. Friedrich's such a baby," says Maya.

Friedrich takes a swing at Maya, who deftly backs away.

"GET IN THE CAR!"

During the ride home, everyone is mad and screaming at one another.

"Friedrich, if you think for a minute that I am ever going to take you anywhere again—"

"I don't give a #%!$."

"Friedrich, you had better watch your mouth."

"I hate Friedrich. I want a new brother. Put him in a foster home."

The main point of this whole example is that sometimes situations don't work out, regardless of whether you might have done everything right or totally screwed things up. Either way, you end up with a disaster on your hands. What to do? Leave disasters behind. End it. Get out of there. Hope tomorrow is better.

And don't worry about trying to teach everybody a lesson they won't forget. Serious repercussions and lengthy lectures only serve to add more unpleasantness to a situation that was already unpleasant enough. Especially if Friedrich does not usually have such tantrums and such behavior was not the rule. But if it's happened before, there is one obvious lesson to be learned—no more miniature golf with Friedrich.

12

Between Parents

Six-year-old Elliot's parents are sitting side by side on the couch. Elliot is cutting up old newspapers with scissors and starting to make a fairly big mess.

"That's enough, Elliot. I want you to pick up all the newspaper and put away the scissors. You're making too much of a mess," said his father.

"But I want to play with the newspapers."

"Elliot, I want you to pick up everything now."

"But I don't want to. I'm not making a mess."

"You *are* making a mess. I told you to pick it up."

"But it's not fair. I'm not making a mess. I'm not."

"Elliot, you heard me. You're looking for trouble."

"But it's not fair."

"Oh, for goodness' sake, Rusty. Let him play with the newspapers. He's not hurting anything. And now he's all upset," said Elliot's mother, growing aggravated with the unfolding scene.

"You stay out of this, Angie. You're always contradicting

me in front of Elliot. He knows if he makes a fuss, you'll always come running to take his side."

"That's not true, Rusty. It's just that you make such unreasonable demands on him. And then the two of you get into these battles. It's awful to have to listen to you."

"Yeah, well, you won't have to listen to me. You win, Elliot. Mommy saved you again." And Elliot's father storms out of the room.

There is a basic rule about two-person parenting. If one parent takes a stand, the other absolutely must back up their partner. To do otherwise undermines the authority of the other parent. Except where there is the threat of physical harm, you should not intervene, even if you disagree. You can make suggestions, perhaps discuss *briefly*, but definitely not in a manner that says either parent might overrule the other one.

"Rusty, he's having such a good time, maybe you could let him play for ten minutes and then he can pick up."

But if the first parent holds firm, you need to back them.

"No, I want Elliot to pick up the mess now."

In which case Elliot's mother should say no more. A parent should only become involved if invited by her or his partner.

"Elliot, pick up the mess!"
"I won't. I won't. It's not a mess. It's not a mess."
"Angie, I am just too tired to deal with him. Will you please handle it?"

Now Angie is in charge.

"Elliot, you can play for ten more minutes, but then I do want you to pick up."

I have always pictured these situations like tag-team wrestling. If one parent wishes the other to take over, no problem. But then the second parent is allowed to decide as they want.

On the other hand, you never want to intervene at the invitation of the child:

"Mommy, I can keep playing, right? I'm not hurting anything, right?"
"Well, he's asking me, Rusty, and I think it's okay."

No. Definitely not.

Angie's only response to Elliot's request must be:

"No. Your father says 'no,' and that's it."

But if not invited to take over, Angie must then let the scene play out without her participation, regardless of the conclusion.

"All you do is yell at me. That's all you do. You just yell at me. You don't let me do anything. You don't."
"I've had it with you, Elliot."

As messily as this scene ends, if Angie had interfered and contradicted her husband, her actions clearly would have caused a number of very real problems.

1. Dissension between parents.

> "Why can't you stay out of it when I'm dealing with Elliot? He's my kid, too, you know. You hate it whenever I try to do anything with him."
> "I would stay out of it if you weren't always so unreasonable with him."
> "You're just spoiling him rotten."

2. Inevitable resentment by the interfered-with parent toward the child.

> Parents will resent a child who regularly runs and turns to the other parent. *He's such a spoiled little brat. All he ever does is run to her all the time.*
> Unfortunately, this can get in the way of a parent's fondness for his or her own child.

3. Rather than relate to a particular parent, a child may simply bypass that parent.

> *I don't have to deal with Daddy. If I don't like what's going on between me and him, I can go to Mommy. Mommy understands me better.*

If Angie routinely undermines the authority of Rusty, the relationship between Rusty and his son is automatically damaged. If Elliot so wishes, he really doesn't have to deal with his father. He can bypass that relationship. On the other hand, if there is no interference, Rusty and Elliot are free to work out their relationship on their own. From Rusty's standpoint, he will have no grudge against Elliot other than what happens between them. The relationship at least has a chance to evolve, for better or worse. But this can happen only where

Elliot and his father can test their relationship unimpeded.

Perhaps the major benefit will be to Elliot. He will have to learn to fend for himself in his relationship with his father, which can be hard when one parent tends to be more harsh. But that's life, sometimes. So long as his father is not truly abusive, Elliot will survive. Since kids desperately want to love and be loved by both of their parents, the great likelihood is that the relationship will come to be a major positive in Elliot's life. But even if Elliot might grow to dislike his father, as sometimes happens, to dislike a father who is not nice is not necessarily bad.

Regardless of the ultimate fate of the relationship, Elliot will feel that, in this special realm of father and son, he managed all on his own. From this he gains a certain self-respect.

I can deal with Dad. I can be with him, take whatever he throws at me, and come out the other end still me. I'm not afraid of him. Sometimes he makes me feel bad, but I can handle it. I am strong.

The general rule is that if you truly disagree with what is going on, if you feel that your partner's overall way of dealing with your child is not good, you can discuss and argue between yourselves as much as you want. But later, when you're by yourselves:

"I think you were too strict with Elliot about his playing. Kids make messes. It wasn't like it was paint or anything. You have to ease up on him. He's just a little kid."

Not that the spouse is likely to agree.

"No, you're the one who's spoiling him. You never say 'no' to him."

But over the course of a childhood, where you genuinely disagree, your words will have an impact, though usually not quite to the degree that you would like.

If there is physical abuse, you *must* intervene to protect your child. If such interference dooms the relationship between the child and abusing parent, so be it. But where it is not physical but only harsh words, the need for intervention from the other parent for the sake of the child is far less clear. Harsh words can damage, but interfering has its risks as well.

If a parent does not intervene directly, he or she can still be of use.

"You little jerk. Don't you have any sense?" says her mother to Antonia.

And later Antonia goes to her father.

"Daddy, am I a jerk? Mom always calls me a jerk."
"No, you're not a jerk. Mom says that because she's mad. But you're not a jerk."

Just these few words can go a long way to restoring self-respect. The child is given significant support in dealing with a verbally harsh parent, but that parent's authority is not undermined.

I'm not a jerk. She only says I'm a jerk. She's a jerk for saying I'm a jerk.

It can take out much of the sting.

Playing One Parent against the Other

"But Daddy said I didn't have to go outside," says Quinlan to his mother. Quinlan's statement is a lie, but at that moment his father is running an errand and unavailable for verification.

When children deviously manipulate their parents to get matters to go their way, they are behaving like normal children. This is what children do. Parents need not worry, because there is a fairly simple and effective response to such deviousness.

1. If the other parent is not there to confirm the child's assertion, then your child is stuck with you.

    "I'm sorry, Quinlan. Your Dad's not here. I want you outside."
    "But it's not fair. Dad said I didn't have to. Wait until he gets home. It's not fair."
    "I'm sorry. I'm here and I want you outside."
    "No, it's not fair."
    "Outside. Now, Quinlan."

2. If the other parent is there, check.

    "Did you say Quinlan didn't have to go outside?"
    "Yeah, it's sort of muddy."

    At that point, the second parent has the option of backing off.

    "Okay, Quinlan. I guess you don't have to go out."
    "Great. You're a great Mom."

Or negotiating:

"Don't you think he should go outside? Otherwise he'll just be in all day and watch TV."

As discussed, the parents can then negotiate *briefly*. The resolution does not matter so long as they decide quickly one way or the other:

"I think your mother is right. You should go outside."
"No, Dad. No. Don't give in to her. Stand up for yourself. You're right. It is muddy."
"Outside, Quinlan."
"I hate both of you." *Cough. Cough.* "I think I have a cold. I can tell it's going to get worse."

3. If a child gets away with the deception and is found out, confront the deviousness.

"Your father did not say you could stay in. You lied, Quinlan. And I don't like that."
"I didn't lie. He said so. He doesn't remember."
"I don't like you being sneaky like that."

The main lesson here for Quinlan is that his parents are in communication. He sees that there is a limit to the success of his deviousness. Should they make a big deal about his sneakiness, his dishonesty, the lying? No, as I discussed at length earlier. In regard to this sort of deviousness, the parents' job is to be on top of it as best as they can. And if once in a while the sneakiness is successful and Quinlan's deviousness is rewarded, so what?

Strict Parent, Easy Parent

Joe:

"I know I'm a lot easier on the kids than Francine. But I think she just expects too much. She's after them all the time about something. I think kids need to be allowed to be kids."

Francine:

"I don't think it's fair. I always have to be the bad guy. The kids know they can get away with anything with their father. But he just doesn't want to take the trouble. I don't think I ask too much. If it was just up to him, I think they'd grow up to be spoiled brats."

The fact is that it simply is not necessary that parents agree about child raising. Usually, at least over some matters, most parents don't agree. Even with quite different philosophies, the disagreement does not have to be a problem. Parents need to back each other, but they do not have to agree.

Most parenting is with only one parent present anyway, and for thousands of years kids have known that they can get away with certain things with one parent and not with the other.

"Mom doesn't care if we put our shoes up on the couch, but Dad does. But if Dad is putting me to bed he always forgets to ask if I brushed my teeth, so I don't."

This is not a problem. And no, children do not love one parent less because he or she is more strict. But yes, they may prefer to go to the movies with one parent rather than the other.

"Mom doesn't let us get candy at all, but Dad lets us get anything. He says it's what his dad who died before I was born used to do with him."

There is a bottom line. It's good that your children have two parents who are involved in their lives. It is what you want. But it also means that neither of you is going to have full control of the raising of your children.

13

Difficult Children

Everything I've said in this book applies to *all* children. But as we all know, some children are easy and some not so easy.

"Noah, would you please put your bike away?"

"But it's not hurting anything."

"Noah, it's blocking the walk, it could get stolen, and it's supposed to rain."

"Nothing's going to happen."

"Noah, please put your bike away."

"But nothing's going to happen. Why do you always make me do stuff? You're always yelling at me to do stuff."

"It's okay, I'll put his bike away when I finish sweeping the walk, Mom," pipes in Seth, Noah's fraternal twin brother.

Some children, through nobody's fault and for any number of reasons, are simply difficult. The following story is one which I have told to a number of parents who have a child considerably more difficult than most. They like the story, knowing its truth, and also knowing that only a parent of a child similar to theirs will ever believe that it could be true.

A mother and her son, Jamie, are in McDonald's. In a booth across from them is a woman with five children who range in age from one to six. The mother of the five children is looking quite harried. The first mother speaks to her and offers a trade. She will take the five children if the mother of five will take her son, Jamie. Overjoyed with her good fortune, the mother of five accepts the trade offer. The children then go home with their new mothers.

Four days later the first mother receives a frantic call from the mother of the five children. "I want my five back; your Jamie is too much."

The ideas discussed in this book do apply to more difficult children and their parents, but they just do not work as well. Yet with these more difficult children, it is even more important that parents not get caught up in all of the baby-self-generated back talk, arguing, case pleading, etc. More difficult children have poorer self-control and seem to have double baby selves. They argue harder and longer. Hence, unless parents want to guarantee that they will become emotionally worn down, they *have* to be more businesslike, avoiding long explanations and speeches intended to teach, which such kids genuinely cannot follow anyway. These parents have to avoid long *anythings*. Unless all interventions are fast, clear, and firm, both child and parent will drown in the conflict.

You must pick your interventions carefully. You may have to ignore shoes on the couch, eating in the family room, slamming the screen door—but not jumping on the couch, which already has weak springs.

There may be different rules within one family.

"You don't ever yell at Reggie for kicking the car seat and you always yell at me. It's not fair."

But rules with children do not have to be the same.

"That's right. I don't yell at Reggie. But I am yelling at you right now. Do not kick the car seat!"

Most important, the parent of a more difficult child simply cannot forget his primary role as nurturer, no matter how trying times may become. These children, regardless how they behave, must know that they are loved and that, even with all their exasperating behavior, they're just as good and valuable as all other children.

I know I act like a brat sometimes. And I wish I could act better. But I just can't stop myself from doing bad stuff. I'd like to be good. I would. I don't want to be bad. I just do a lot of bad stuff.

Such children are enormously gratified and relieved if it is understood by their parents that in their hearts they are good. It is easy for parents and the children themselves to lose sight of this. This loss of perspective, more than anything else, can lead to future trouble. Instead, we want them to know:

I am good. It's just that often I don't act that way.

If parents can survive their difficult child's childhood and, while doing so, somehow communicate that though their child is difficult—no question about that—he or she is no less good, no less loved, they have done well, indeed.

ADD/ADHD

Many of these more difficult children are now described as having ADD, Attention Deficit Disorder. In 1980, when the American Psychiatric Association published its third official diagnostic manual of all the different psychiatric disorders — known as DSM III — the categories of psychiatric problems for children were considerably changed from the previous manual. Very significantly, a category for hyperactivity disorder was deleted and a new category added. The new category was called Attention Deficit Disorder (ADD).

ADD was not presented as a disease like Asian flu or measles. That is, it was not tied to any specific cause or specific change inside the body. Rather ADD was simply presented as a description of behaviors that seemed to fit a large group of kids (about four times as many boys as girls). Furthermore, this new category was broken down into two types of ADD: with or without hyperactivity. (The next official diagnostic manual renamed it ADHD — Attention Deficit Hyperactivity Disorder. Then a subsequent manual went back to ADD — mainly hyperactive, mainly inattentive, or mixed.)

The main feature of ADD with hyperactivity is that these children are far more active than other children their age — more impulsive, with significantly greater difficulty paying attention to and staying with activities that require sustained concentration, especially schoolwork.

The ADD diagnosis dramatically changed the face of child psychiatry. As a diagnostic category, it has one very unusual characteristic. It is the first child diagnosis that many parents *want* their children to have. Nobody realized that this would be the effect of this new category, but this is indeed what happened. Why? Because the diagnosis said to parents that their child's wild and often disobedient behavior and poor performance in school were not caused either by poor parenting or by a "bad attitude." Suddenly "bad" parenting and/or their "bad" child were looked at in a whole new light. The new category said to parents, *It is not your fault.*

The effect was quite swift: *Lots* of kids started being diagnosed with ADD/ADHD. Something else happened. For many years prior to 1980, certain stimulant medications—basically Ritalin, Dexedrine, and Cylert—had been prescribed for hyperactive kids. They seemed to produce significant changes for the better. With the official recognition of the ADD/ADHD diagnosis, the use of these medications, especially Ritalin, exploded.

All in all, I believe the official recognition of ADD/ADHD is to the good. Is ADD/ADHD too readily and too quickly diagnosed today? Probably. Is medication prescribed too quickly or inappropriately as a solution for problem behaviors? Probably. But there is no question that medication (currently a number of different medications) seems to produce noticeable changes in many children, who seem to have themselves under better control and seem to be able to focus more in school and perform better.

How do you know if a given child with ADD-type behaviors should be on medication? As a psychologist and not a medical doctor, I do not make recommendations regarding whether a child should or should not be on medication. Rather, based on my observations over the years with children who have been on medication, I tell parents how I would view it as a parent.

There are basically four categories of problems for which I would think about medication *if* other kinds of interventions did not seem to produce significant change. In this case, I would take the matter to the next step, which is to talk with a medical doctor such as a psychiatrist, pediatrician, pediatric neurologist, or psychopharmacologist, who does deal with medication. I would ask what he or she thought, find out about any possible side effects, and then decide.

The four problems are:

1. If the problem behavior seems to interfere significantly either with my child's ability to learn or to complete schoolwork. This can only be determined over time. A bad week or a bad month isn't indicative. Consult with your child's school to determine if there is a continuing discrepancy between what he accomplishes in school and his actual intellectual ability, as best as you can judge it (and here testing is definitely useful).
2. If the problem behavior jeopardizes your child's ability to stay in a regular classroom, or if teachers (plural, not just one teacher) continually say that your child's behavior interferes too much with their ability to manage the classroom.
3. If your child's behavior at home creates such a constant and high level of stress that you and/or your partner are pushed to feeling out of control, or if most of the time you truly hate being with your own child.
4. If your child's behavior constantly alienates all peers, is simply "too wild" for them to tolerate, with the result that your child has no friends.

If any of these four apply, I would *consider* medication. On the other hand, many children who probably fit into the ADD category seem able to manage without medication. They seem able to adequately channel their extra energy and their impulsiveness and are able to keep up in school, have friends, do well in sports (this is often the case), and not make their home a hellish place to be.

Therefore the most relevant question in regard to ADD is probably not, Does my child have ADD? The better question is: are the symptoms that are leading me to wonder if my child has ADD significantly getting in the way of his or her being able to have a happy, productive childhood?

Conclusion:
Giving Them a Childhood

Our children are more seed than clay. They are themselves, their own little genetic package growing into whom they will become. As parents we can add our piece, put in the ingredients of parenting—love, attention, encouragement, setting limits, making demands—but we will not be able to shape them exactly as we wish. It simply does not work that way. What we as parents do is important, hugely important, but it is also limited. Beyond the sum total of our input—good or bad—remain forces that shape who they become and over which we have no control at all. Children take their own form. We can only put in what we feel are the best ingredients, and then hope.

In truth there is a special problem in parenting one's own kids. We care so much. We would be much more dispassionate, much better in control of ourselves were we raising other people's kids. Because we love them so much, because we are so close to them, they easily pull out our baby self. But they also pull out from us what is probably the best that we have to give—what is truly selfless, caring not for ourselves, not for our pride, not for what we get out of it, but for them. But this does make us so vulnerable moment by moment when things don't seem to be going well, not the way we planned, not on the path that seems to lead to their best possible future success and happiness. With our kids we care so much.

But that same vulnerability translates into something on which our kids thrive. They know. For better or for worse, to us they are very special.

What do I want for my children? That they have a childhood. That so long as nobody gets hurt, there will be a place that is theirs, in which they are always okay. I may stop them. I may tell them how obnoxious they are being. At times I may even deposit them somewhere else. But I do no more. And if in my heart, even when I do not like what they are doing and clearly let them know, I also truly and deeply believe that whatever it is that they are doing is okay—they will hear this, too. They will hear that with me there is this place, their childhood—that I do want them to have—a place where they are never bad, a place that is always safe and worry-free. A place of absolute nurturing.

And children who have been given this place do not grow up to be wild or disrespectful or to take advantage of others. Just the opposite. They become people who can give, care about others, and make the world in which they live a better place for their being in it.

And if a parent truly believes that giving a child this place—a childhood—is what is best, it turns out that that belief is a great aid in child raising. That it can make child raising so much easier and so much more pleasant.

For if parents truly believe that all the obnoxious, bratty, selfish behavior that they get is really not a big deal, that it is baby-self behavior and nothing more, and if they want to make a place for the baby self, then parents will feel much less of a need to respond to all of the nonsense that the baby self throws at them when it is not getting its way. In turn, much of the baby self's most obnoxious behavior is eliminated. In other words, if I can allow them a childhood, they will give me the joy of being a parent.